point of grace

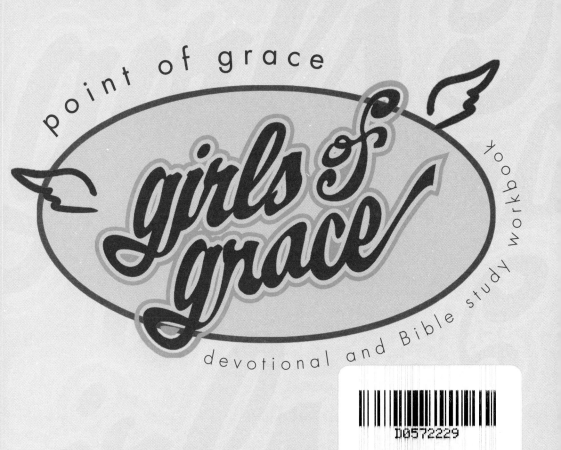

girls of grace

devotional and Bible study workbook

HOWARD
PUBLISHING CO.

Our purpose at Howard Publishing is to:

- *Increase faith* in the hearts of growing Christians
- *Inspire holiness* in the lives of believers
- *Instill hope* in the hearts of struggling people everywhere

   Because He's coming again!

Published by Howard Publishing Co., Inc.
3117 North 7th Street, West Monroe, Louisiana 71291-2227

   04 05 06 07 08 09 10 11   20 19 18 17 16 15 14 13 12

Study Guides by Whitney Prosperi
Edited by Philis Boultinghouse
Interior design by Stephanie Denney
Cover design by LinDee Loveland
Cover photos by Robert Ascroft/Industrie Rep

Photography on pages 1, 41, 51, 97, 105, 147, 189 by Robert Ascroft/Industrie Rep
Photography on pages 23, 87 by Michael Haber

ISBN: 1-58229-268-X

Excerpt in chapter 1: Donald Whitney, *Spiritual Disciplines for the Christian Life* (Colorado Springs, Colo.: NavPress, 1997), pp. 15–16. Used by permission. All rights reserved.

Contents

Foreword by Beth Moore

What a perfect time to share a few words about my sisters in Point Of Grace! I had the opportunity to minister with them only last night. As we "gathered 'round the river," my memory rewound an entire decade to the very same church where I first saw them. Long before "Point Of Grace" was a household name in countless Christian homes, Heather, Denise, Terry, and Shelley came to one of my Bible studies as special guest singers. They were students at Ouachita Baptist University at the time, and I doubt that the word *artists* had ever occurred to them. When they opened their mouths, God opened His heavens, and the rest—as they say—is history.

I was only one of many who got to sit on the sidelines for the years that followed and watch God be huge. I'll never forget how I felt when they accepted their first Dove Award. I wept over the privilege of getting to witness such an amazing work of God from such close proximity.

Foreword by Beth Moore

Acts 17:26–27 reads, "From one man He made every nation of men, that they should inhabit the whole earth; and He determined the times set for them and the exact places where they should live. God did this so that men would seek Him and perhaps reach out for Him and find Him, though He is not far from each one of us" (NIV). Whenever I teach these verses, I use Heather, Denise, Terry, and Shelley as the perfect examples of a God who tailor designs servants for specific generations.

Can you picture Point Of Grace in our great, great grandmother's churches? Hardly! *Revival* would have taken on a whole new meaning as much of the congregation required CPR. But our generation? I can't think of anyone God has suited more perfectly to minister to His people in our day. I am convinced that some of their greatest works are ahead.

I have celebrated every work Point Of Grace has accomplished, but I can honestly say I have never been more exited than I am about Girls Of Grace. God has given these four young women favor among girls of all ages, and I am thrilled by their determination to be good stewards of their positions of influence.

You are going to love *Girls Of Grace!* You're also going to want to grab a copy for every girl you know. This book has the Spirit-empowered capacity to change young lives. It's about time this generation grasped that nothing is cooler than being a Christian.

Ten years ago, as those four college girls sauntered onto that stage, I was quite sure I had never seen a more precious gathering of fresh faces in all my life. Then last night…I thought the same thing. Grace lasts. That's all there is to it.

A friend loves at all times,
and a brother is born for adversity.
Proverbs 17:17 NIV

Introduction

Over the years we have been blessed to meet teenage girls from all across the country. No matter where these girls live or what kind of life circumstance they find themselves in, they all struggle with some of the same basic issues.

First Timothy 4:12 says, "Let no one look down on your youthfulness, but rather in speech, conduct, love, faith, and purity, show yourself an example of those who believe" (NASB). The truth is, applying this verse at any age is difficult, but it is especially hard during the teenage years. As we talk with teenage girls, we see that they really are striving to glorify God in their lives, but they have many questions about life that desperately need to be answered.

So, to all of you precious girls who are looking for answers, this book is our attempt to encourage you in your faith, to challenge you in your walk with Christ, and to aid you in your search for answers to many of life's questions.

Introduction

In writing this book, we have come to realize more than ever that we do not have all the answers. But we are intimately acquainted with our Mighty God who does hold all the answers. We prayed and studied and sought God's guidance as we wrote the words on the pages of this book.

We ask that you open your hearts as we share what God has placed on our hearts for you. Our hope is that the Lord will use this book to minister to you right where you are. Our prayer for you is that you know you are loved and that the "God of our Lord Jesus Christ, the glorious Father, may give you the Spirit of wisdom and revelation, so that you may know Him better. We pray also that the eyes of your heart may be enlightened in order that you may know the hope to which He has called you, the riches of His glorious inheritance in the saints, and His incomparably great power for us who believe" (Ephesians 1:17–19 NIV).

With all our hearts,

Heather

faith

Dear Point Of Grace,

I don't seem to have time for anything anymore. When I first became a Christian, I loved reading my Bible and having a quiet time every day, but with school, track, piano lessons—plus all the chores I'm expected to do—there aren't enough hours in the day for devotionals anymore. And when I'm finally to the point where I have some free time, I just don't feel like reading something so serious. Is it that important to read the Bible every day? I go to church every Sunday and Wednesday. Can't I just learn enough about Jesus and God that way?

What do you think?

Megan

*No discipline seems pleasant at the
time, but painful. Later on, however,
it produces a harvest of righteousness and
peace for those who have been trained by it.*
Hebrews 12:11 NIV

What's So Good about *Discipline?*

"Have you finished your homework?" "Did you clean your room?" "Don't forget to practice the piano." "Yes, you have to eat all of your peas." Does any of this sound familiar? Well, it sure does to me, and I remember all too clearly my responses as I huffed and puffed and rolled my eyes on my way to do whatever I was told. However, what I thought was a total pain at the time, I now see was for my own good. It was all a lesson in discipline.

By *discipline* I don't mean punishment; I mean training or instruction. That's what my parents were trying to do with all their questions and rules: They were training me, teaching me how to live life responsibly. You see, what we don't understand as teenagers—and what our parents already know—is that much of what we learn as young people will establish who we become as adults. I recently read this story in a book called *Spiritual Disciplines of the Christian Life* by Donald Whitney. He writes:

3

Imagine six-year-old Kevin, whose parents have enrolled him in music lessons. After school every afternoon, he sits in the living room and reluctantly strums "Home on the Range" while watching his buddies play baseball in the park across the street. That's discipline without direction. It's drudgery.

Now suppose Kevin is visited by an angel one afternoon during guitar practice. In a vision he's taken to Carnegie Hall. He's shown a guitar virtuoso giving a concert. Usually bored by classical music, Kevin is astonished by what he sees and hears. The musician's fingers dance excitedly on the strings with fluidity and grace. Kevin thinks of how stupid and klunky his hands feel when they halt and stumble over the chords. The virtuoso blends clean, soaring notes into a musical aroma that wafts from his guitar. Kevin remembers the toneless, irritating discord that comes stumbling out of his.

But Kevin is enchanted. His head tilts slightly to one side as he listens. He drinks in everything. He never imagined that anyone could play the guitar like this. "What do you think, Kevin?" asks the angel. The answer is a soft, six-year-old's "Wow!" The vision vanishes, and the angel is again standing in front of Kevin in his living room. "Kevin," says the angel, "the wonderful musician you saw is you in a few years." Then pointing at the guitar, the angel declares, "But you must practice!"

I love that story. Now put yourself in Kevin's place. What is the first thing you would do when the angel left? Well, you would practice, of course. Why?

What's So Good about *Discipline?*

Because you would now have a vision of your very own. You would know what you were going to become; you would have a *reason* to be disciplined.

God has a goal in mind for us that is very important to Him. His goal is that we be "conformed to the image of His Son" (Romans 8:29 NASB). But there's a catch. In order for us to make God's goal our own and become like His Son, we must know Jesus intimately. And that takes time and discipline. The primary way we get to know Him is through His Word.

Proverbs 2:6 says, "For the LORD gives wisdom, and from His mouth come knowledge and understanding" (NIV). The Bible is God's inspired Word, and it is the tool He has given us to get to know Him and learn from Him. Second Timothy 3:16–17 says, "All Scripture is God-breathed and is useful for teaching, rebuking, correcting and training in righteousness, so that the man of God may be thoroughly equipped for every good work" (NIV). The more time we spend in His Word, the more we will know Him and His holy character. This is how we begin to fulfill God's goal for us to become like Jesus. If our hearts are in line with God's, we will want to have the same goals for ourselves that He does.

First Timothy 4:7 says, "Discipline yourself for the purpose of godliness" (NASB). The Greek word for "discipline" is *gumnasia,* and you can probably guess what it means. It translates into our English words *gymnasium* or *gymnastics,* and it means "to exercise or discipline." Spending time with God every day is considered spiritual exercise. In order to have a healthy spiritual life, we must discipline—or exercise—ourselves daily in Bible reading and prayer.

Faith—Heather

As a young teenager, I was challenged to begin having a personal devotional or quiet time with God every day. During the first few weeks, it was really hard to make the time. But I was determined, and so every day I would read the Bible, pray, and write in my journal. Before I knew it, my time with God was a regular part of my day. As I finished high school, then college, and now in my adult life, I see my time with God as a *necessity*. Only by spending time with Him am I able to walk in the Spirit and respond to things in a godly way. I thank God that someone made the effort to challenge me in this way. Regular time with God is the most enriching and rewarding experience in my life.

And now I would like to extend the same challenge to you. If you accept this challenge and regularly make time for Him in your life, you will be blessed beyond your dreams. And once you make time with Him a habit, you'll find that if you neglect your quiet time, you will miss Him immensely. The fact of the matter is that you desperately need God. God is the life-giver and the One who nurtures your soul and lavishes His amazing love on you each day. Going about your day without making Him part of it is saying to Him that you don't need Him.

Once, when Jesus was asked which of the commandments was the greatest, he quickly replied: "You shall love the Lord your God with all your heart, and with all your soul, and with all your mind. This is the great and foremost commandment" (Matthew 22:37–38 NASB). Do you love Him like that? If not, wouldn't you like to? You can if you get in the Word. When you love

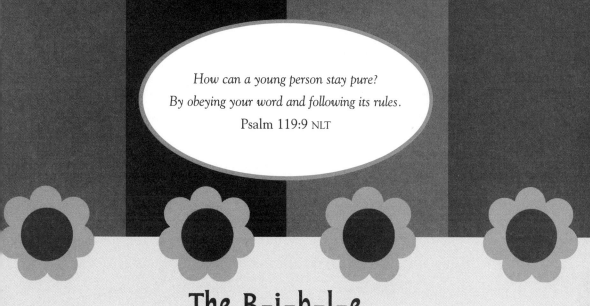

The B-i-b-l-e

One of the very first songs I ever learned was "The B-i-b-l-e." Remember that song? "The B-i-b-l-e, yes, that's the book for me. I stand alone on the Word of God, the B-i-b-l-e." I love that song. As a matter of fact, I've heard Denise's son Spence sing it a few times, and I must say that every time I hear it, it brings back memories of going to vacation Bible school and Sunday school.

I'll never forget the day I got my first Bible. It was white and had beautifully colored pictures in it. I felt very grown up when I carried it to church for the first time. I grew up knowing that the Bible was God's Word and that it was a very important book. Now that I am older, and maybe even a little wiser, I see that reading the Bible is not just important—it is vital to the Christian walk.

I heard my husband say recently that the Bible is God's thoughts to us.

I like that idea. In addition to giving us insight into how God *thinks*, the Bible is the primary way that God *speaks* to us. His Word teaches us how to live a life that pleases Him and glorifies His name. Second Peter 1:3 says that "as we know Jesus better, His divine power gives us everything we need for living a godly life" (NLT). The way we get to "know Jesus better" is by reading and studying the Bible.

You know, it's not easy to live life the way God wants us to. How can you stand up against the temptations and difficulties of this life? How can you be the friend God calls you to be? How can you be an obedient daughter and a kind sister? How can you behave purely and righteously when you're out with a guy you really like and don't want to lose? God knows that you face these difficult questions. The writer of Psalm 119 asks the very same kind of question—and he gives you the answer: "How can a young person stay pure? By obeying your word and following its rules" (verse 9 NLT). You can't very well obey God's Word and follow its rules if you don't know what it says. Spending time in His Word is a key ingredient to keeping yourself pure.

You may be thinking, *I'm only a teenager. What's the rush? I'll make time for it when I'm older.* Let me tell you a story that will demonstrate why it's so important to start now. Not long ago, my husband and I and a friend of ours were out making random door-to-door visits. (We're part of a Tuesday-night evangelism/visitation group.) We ended up visiting with two young men who were college students. The first young man graciously invited us in. As we sat down, I was horrified to see a pornographic magazine sitting right on top of the coffee table. We began to ask him questions about his life, and it saddened me deeply to find out that he was raised in church. He knew all the right answers to our questions about what it took to go to heaven, but he pretty much admitted that he was a party animal. He said that he'd never been into reading the Bible but that if he ever started feeling bad about how he was living, he would pick it up. My husband, Brian, was very bold in his response to him but also very kind. As we left my heart was aching, and I couldn't say a word as we walked to our next house.

The young man at this house also invited us in, and lo and behold, sitting right there on the coffee table was yet another pornographic magazine. I was thankful that he removed the magazine as we sat down to visit with him. Like the first young man, he also told us that he had grown up in church, and he, too, answered all of our questions correctly. He also knew that he wasn't living right. But this guy was different; it was obvious that he was miserable in his sin. We prayed with him and invited him to the college service at our church and asked him if there was anything that we could do for him. He told us that he wasn't very familiar with the Bible and asked if we could give him some scriptures to read—which, of course, Brian did.

Now, what do you see in this scenario? Both of these young men were raised in the church, yet neither had ever established a habit of reading their Bibles regularly. However, they both recognized the Bible as the book to go to when they felt bad about their lifestyles.

Here is what I see, my friend. It is not enough to go to church. One sermon on Sunday, no matter how good it is, will not supply you with the strength you need for every day of the week. I don't know about you, but I need God daily. I need Him every second of every minute.

In 2 Timothy 3 the apostle Paul writes to his young friend and disciple Timothy and tells him: "Remain faithful to the things you have been taught. You know they are true, for you know you can trust those who taught you. You have been taught the holy Scriptures from childhood, and they have given you the wisdom to receive the salvation that comes by trusting in Christ Jesus" (verses 14–15 NLT). We see from this passage that Timothy began learning from the Word of God when he was a child. Then in verses 16 and 17, Paul tells Timothy why spending time with God's Word is so important: "All Scripture is inspired by God and profitable for *teaching*, for *reproof*, for *correction*, for *training* in righteousness; so that the man of God may be adequate, equipped for every good work" (NASB). I like what Warren Wiersbe says in his commentary on verse 16. He says that we need *teaching* to learn what *is* right, we need *reproof* to learn what is *not* right, we need *correction* to learn how to *be* right, and we need *training* in righteousness to learn how to *stay* right.

This passage is the summation of why we need the Bible and why it is essential for our growth as godly young women.

Now, I promised you in the last devotional that I'd try to do more than just tell you *what* to do and actually tell you *how* to do it. Well, here are a few different ideas to get you started in your daily Bible reading.

Daily devotional books. There are numerous daily devotional books out there. When I first started having a quiet time, I used one called *Our Daily*

Bread. It had a Scripture reading every day and then a devotional thought based on the passage that you read. Devotional books can be very helpful; just be careful not to depend more on what the devotional writer says than what the Bible says.

The Book of Proverbs. You may know this already, but there are thirty-one chapters in the Book of Proverbs—one for each day of the month. I have read a chapter a day for years. When you finish, you can start right over again. Honestly, it never gets old.

The Book of Psalms. The Book of Psalms has 150 chapters. You can read a psalm a day for five months. I love reading the psalms.

The whole Bible. I challenge you to set the goal of reading the Bible all the way through. It may sound overwhelming, but you can take your time. It takes a while, and there are some difficult passages, but it is altogether a wonderful experience. You might try an easy-to-read version like the New Living Translation. This translation is more accurate than a "paraphrase," and it's easier to read than some of the other versions.

The "how" of reading the Bible every day can be different for everyone. You'll find that the more you read the Bible on a daily basis, the more you will work out your own system of doing it. What is important is that you do it and that you do it consistently.

In Isaiah 55 God speaks beautifully about His Word. I love this passage: "The rain and snow come down from the heavens and stay on the ground to water the earth. They cause the grain to grow, producing seed for the farmer and bread for the hungry. It is the same with my word. I send it out, and it always produces fruit. It will accomplish all I want it to, and it will prosper everywhere I send it" (verses 10–11 NLT).

What does this mean? It means that God, through His Word, gives us all we need. He nourishes us, He gives us strength, and He equips us to live a godly life and minister the good news of the gospel of Jesus Christ to others.

My friend, reading God's Word and spending time with Him consistently are the most important parts of becoming a godly young woman. I pray that you will make them consistent parts of your life. And I promise that, if you do, you will be richly rewarded.

For God did not give us a spirit of timidity,
but a spirit of power, of love and of self-discipline.
2 Timothy 1:7 NIV

What's a "Spiritual Discipline"?

Have you ever heard anyone talk about "spiritual disciplines" and wondered what on earth they were talking about? No, it doesn't mean some kind of *cosmic punishment*. Far from it. Spiritual disciplines are habits that we practice regularly to help us grow spiritually. They include habits like meditating on (thinking about) God's Word, reading and studying your Bible, and spending quiet alone-time with God. There are many spiritual disciplines that help us live the abundant Christian life, but I want to concentrate on three that have been an important part of deepening my walk with God—*praying, journaling,* and *memorizing Scripture.* These three practices, more than anything else, have enhanced my relationship with God.

Prayer. One summer at youth camp, a friend of mine wrote in my Bible "JE-333: God's phone number." Now, honestly, at first I had no idea what that meant, but I finally realized that he wrote it in the margin of Jeremiah 33:3, which says, "Call to Me, and I will answer you, and I will tell you great and mighty things, which you do not know" (NASB). Now, I don't know that I would use the "God's phone number" thing, but the point of the verse is prayer, and I always want to use that.

Now, when I talk about prayer, I'm talking about more than the prayers you pray with other people listening in. In Matthew 6:6 Jesus says, "When you pray, go away by yourself, shut the door behind you, and pray to your Father secretly. Then your Father, who knows all secrets, will reward you" (NLT). I gather from this verse that prayer is personal and private and that it's important to get alone with God. Of course I pray publicly and with my husband and intimate friends and family, but my deepest prayer life is a "closet" thing.

And prayer is more than asking God for things—even when we're asking for other people. Prayer is also about getting to know God. In the book *Becoming a Woman of Prayer,* Cynthia Heald wrote: "Often my prayer is for God to show me how to please Him. I think in terms of active doing with people, but God receives pleasure from our wanting to be with Him." Can you identify with Cynthia? I can. I, too, sometimes get all wrapped up in doing things for and with *people,* when God wants me to spend time with *Him.*

I love what Oswald Chambers said about prayer in his devotional *My Utmost for His Highest:* "When a man is born from above, the life of the Son of God is born in him, and he can either starve that life or nourish it. Prayer is the way the life of God is nourished. We look upon prayer as a means of getting things for ourselves; the Bible's idea of prayer is that we may get to know God Himself." Some days, I have a hard time getting started in my prayer—

What's a "Spiritual Discipline"?

I just can't find the words. Perhaps God is encouraging me to nourish the "life of the Son of God" in me. Maybe He just wants me to be still and get to know Him. We were created for fellowship with God, and prayer is a beautiful way to have that fellowship with Him.

OK, now that we've talked a little about what prayer is, let me share with you a couple of "how-tos." The first is a formula I learned when I was growing up. You may already know it: It's based on the word ACTS.

- *A is for adoration*, which is praising God and telling Him how truly awesome He is and how much you love Him.
- *C is for confession*. When you confess your sins to God, be as specific as you possibly can. If you'll do this, you'll start seeing what you repeatedly confess, and you'll be more aware of your weakness and better able to ask for God's help. And make sure that you not only confess but also repent of, or turn away from, your sin.
- *T is for thanksgiving*. Thank the Lord for all the many blessings that He gives you daily. Again, be specific, because not only does it bless God's heart, it opens your eyes to how great He is.
- *S is for supplication*. Supplication is humbly asking God to help you with your personal needs and the needs of others.

Another very powerful way to pray is to pray Scripture. What could be more powerful than praying God's inspired Word back to the One who inspired it?

Here's an example based on Psalm 27:1 which says, "The LORD is my light and my salvation—so why should I be afraid? The LORD protects me from danger—so why should I tremble?" (NLT). Here's how you can pray this back to God:

Lord, you are my light, and light does away with darkness. You light my path and make things clear. You are my salvation; You have saved me from my sin. You are my protector from all danger. So, Lord, I have no reason to fear, because You have promised that You will never leave me or forsake me. I am so grateful that you came into my heart and made me whole and secure and safe. I am so thankful that you are there.

Praying God's Word is not hard, and it is very rewarding. I'd like to recommend two books that can help you learn to pray the Scriptures: Donald Whitney's book *Spiritual Disciplines for the Christian Life* and Beth Moore's book *Praying God's Word*. Now let's look at another spiritual discipline.

Journaling. When I talk about journaling, I'm really talking about a specific way of praying. I have been journaling since I was in junior high, except back then I called it writing in my diary. There is something very freeing about writing your thoughts to God. When I journal, I tell God my thoughts and dreams and fears and successes. Oh, I know that He already knows these things, but it has always been good for me to write them out. Some days I may write one sentence, and on other days I may take up several pages, writing from the very depth of my soul.

Only God knows what is in the pages of my journals. When I think about journaling, I often think about the psalmist David and how so many of his psalms sound like journal entries written to the Lord. David writes about his struggles and about his times of rejoicing. I can identify with much of what he writes. I bet you can, too.

If you had asked me ten years ago if I would ever share something I had written in my journal, I would have said "No way!" However, when I was preparing to write this devotional, I spent time reading through some of my old journals, and it was such a wonderful experience that I thought I would share an entry with you.

Tuesday, October 13, 1992. Bless the Lord, O my soul. All that is within me, bless His Holy name. Oh, Lord, You are so faithful. Thank You for revealing and teaching me that nothing is impossible with You. The key is "with You." I need Your presence in every second of every day.

As you know, Lord, there are days that my heart is discontent. I pray that You will help me learn from Moses and the children of Israel that, even when my circumstances are bleak and I think I can't go on, You are with me. You are my provider, and it does not please You when I complain.

Lord, I know that You meet my every need, but sometimes I doubt because You don't meet my need the way I think You should; but no matter what, You are faithful to care for me. Forgive me for my moments of discontent and doubt. I will count my trials as joy, and I will not lose heart at doing good. And, Father, with Your strength, I will not grow weary.

Lord, carry me through this day and help me glorify You in all that I say and do. Thank you for Your everlasting, unchanging love.

Faith—Heather

Reading back through my journal, I am amazed at how much I've changed through the years. My life has been a bit of a roller coaster, and most of those ups and downs are written in the pages of my journals. The thing that leaves me awestruck is that the one thing that never changed in all my years of journal entries is the presence of God. He was and is always there, and as I read through the pages of my life, I was so encouraged to see His faithfulness.

Today, I want to encourage you to begin journaling. I promise that when you look back years later, you, too, will be amazed at how actively involved God is in your life.

Scripture memorization. Finally, a truly vital spiritual discipline is memorizing Scripture. Doing this will help you grow in intimacy with God and will help you be more effective in living out His will for your life. Most of you have probably memorized a verse here and there, but have you ever memorized an entire psalm or a long passage of Scripture? I have to be honest with you: It wasn't until I married Brian that I began to memorize more than one verse of Scripture.

Before I was challenged by Brian, I had always claimed that I didn't have a very good memory. But I finally figured out that when it comes to things I love, like movie actors and fashion and music, I remember just fine. This realization convicted me, and I started memorizing passages of Scripture. It is amazing how the passages I commit to memory pop up in my mind just when I need them. Whether I am being tempted or am presented with a ministry opportunity, God's words are much more powerful than my own.

What's a "Spiritual Discipline"?

Psalm 119:11 says, "I have hidden your word in my heart, that I might not sin against you" (NIV). Just think how much of God's Word will live in you when you are an adult if you'll start memorizing Scripture now.

Let me share some tactics that have helped me in this discipline.

- Write the verses you are memorizing on Post-it notes, and stick them in several places where you will see them during the day.
- Write your memory verses in your journal. It always helps to write them down.
- Find a friend who will memorize along with you and keep you accountable. You could even offer each other incentives like saying that whoever finishes last has to treat the other to a meal.
- Say the verses over and over in your mind right before you go to bed. While you sleep, you may unconsciously think about these verses because that was the last thing you thought about before you went to bed. And who knows—it might even be the first thing you think about in the morning.

The neat thing about all three of these disciplines is how they work together. You can write your prayers to God and the verses you want to memorize in your journal. Then you can use the verses that you've memorized to pray God's Word in your personal prayer time.

My heart's desire is that you find the joy in these spiritual disciplines that I have. I pray for you what the apostle Paul prayed for the Christians in the city of Ephesus: I ask "God, the glorious Father of our Lord Jesus Christ, to give you spiritual wisdom and understanding, so that you might grow in your knowledge of God. I pray that your hearts will be flooded with light so that you can understand the wonderful future he has promised to those he called. I want you to realize what a rich and glorious inheritance he has given to his people. I pray that you will begin to understand the incredible greatness of his power for us who believe him" (Ephesians 1:17–19 NLT).

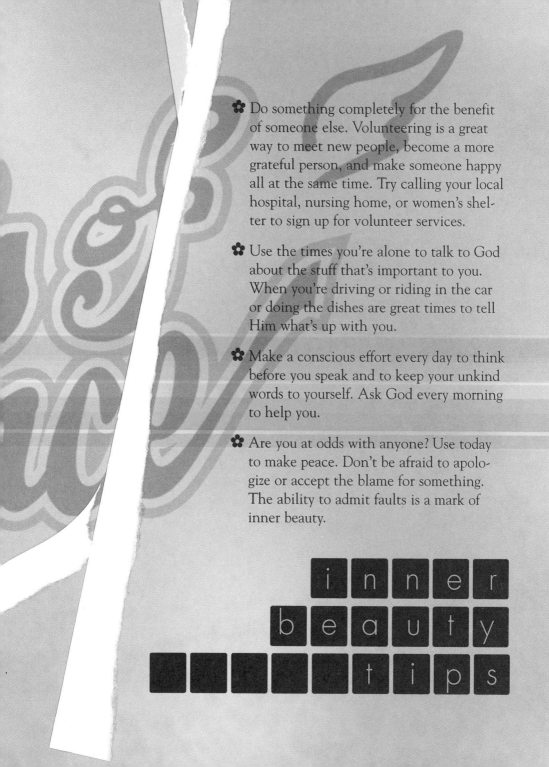

✿ Do something completely for the benefit of someone else. Volunteering is a great way to meet new people, become a more grateful person, and make someone happy all at the same time. Try calling your local hospital, nursing home, or women's shelter to sign up for volunteer services.

✿ Use the times you're alone to talk to God about the stuff that's important to you. When you're driving or riding in the car or doing the dishes are great times to tell Him what's up with you.

✿ Make a conscious effort every day to think before you speak and to keep your unkind words to yourself. Ask God every morning to help you.

✿ Are you at odds with anyone? Use today to make peace. Don't be afraid to apologize or accept the blame for something. The ability to admit faults is a mark of inner beauty.

inner
beauty
tips

Shelley

faMily

Dear Point Of Grace,

My parents are driving me crazy! They are so strict and so out of it! They don't let me hang out in the places most of my friends are allowed to go to. They insist on knowing where I'm going, who I'm going with, and what I'm doing every second of the day. And then I have to call them if my plans change or if I'm going to be late. And all of this leads to fights—lots of them. I don't remember a weekend in the last year when we didn't end up yelling at each other. I want a better relationship with my parents, but they just don't get it! Can you help?

Natalia

Honor your father and your mother,
so that you may live long in the land
the LORD your God is giving you.
Exodus 20:12 NIV

Honor Your Father and Mother

I wish I could say that I followed the advice I'm about to give you, but the fact of the matter is—I didn't. Don't get me wrong, I wasn't a bad teenager. I didn't drink or do drugs, but I did have a famously smart mouth.

To be completely honest, my relationship with God as a teenager was spotty at best. Sometimes I was very diligent in my devotionals and disciplined in my prayer life, but at other times I was just plain disinterested. This is probably why I wasn't as respectful of my mom and dad as I should have been.

I don't think I fought with my mom and dad any more or any less than the average teenage girl, but now it occurs to me that God doesn't call us to be average teenagers but to live our lives by a higher standard. (My mom's probably thinking, *Too bad that didn't occur to you when you were thirteen, smarty-pants.*)

Ephesians 5:1–2 talks of this higher standard—the notion of modeling our actions after Christ. It says, "Be *imitators* of God, therefore, as dearly loved children and live a life of love, just as Christ loved us and gave himself up for us" (NIV). Hmm…"imitators of God." That concept will change the way you react to your parents real quick—if you really take it to heart.

I'm here to tell you that following two simple concepts will instantly strengthen your relationship with your mom and dad and, more important, will please your heavenly parent—God. Now, I don't use the word *simple* as in "easy," but *simple* as in "basic and foundational." These two concepts are *honor* and *obedience*.

So what does honor mean, anyway? In the context of Exodus 20:12, "Honor your father and mother" means to hold them in high esteem and respect. And by obedience, I mean being a big enough person to accept what your parents say and obey them whether you agree or not. (Ugh! That's a hard one!)

I totally understand that it's hard to honor your parents when you want to do something they don't want you to do. Can I tell you how uncool I felt when I wasn't allowed to go to 8 Wheels on Friday nights as a teenager? "What is 8 wheels?" you might ask. Well, it was only the *only* place to be on Friday nights when I was in the seventh grade. As much as I wanted to be with the kids I perceived to be the coolest seventh-graders in town, my parents wouldn't let me. They didn't think a seventh-grade girl should be dropped off by herself at a roller-skating rink where older kids were hanging out and you could come and go as you please. Honestly, looking back, I can

Honor Your Father and Mother

see they were right. It was a rather "seedy" place, but I didn't see it that way then. See? I had different eyes then.

Then, in the eighth grade, the "cool" people moved on to Star Systems. Now *that* was the ultimate place to be. It was *much* cooler than 8 Wheels. It was a dark video arcade in an outdoor strip mall, and it was completely unsupervised. Let's just say, some "not so great stuff" went on outside that arcade. As my luck would have it, just about the time that 8 Wheels was out and Star Systems was in, Mom and Dad said I could go to the roller rink, but then it was too late—it just wasn't cool anymore. My friends had "moved on."

I remember what seemed like endless Friday nights, crying to my parents, pleading with them to let me go where my friends were going—yelling, smarting off, or whatever I thought would convince them to let me go. Of course, none of my tactics worked. Now I understand that it wasn't necessarily *me* they didn't trust, but simply the potential dangers of the situations. In reality, they were protecting me.

You're probably thinking, *8 Wheels? Star Systems? How completely ridiculous and insignificant, how completely lame!* This, my sweet friend, is *exactly* my point! What then seemed like the hugest deal in the world is absolutely meaningless now. If I had taken the time to step back and look at the situation realistically, it would have changed the way I reacted. How much better would it have been if I'd simply obeyed my parents? That's right, honor and obey—maybe even cheerfully. Obedience and respect actually bring better long-term results than do whining and fighting. That kind of maturity can actually make your parents trust and respect you more.

This may sound a little cheesy, but if my attitude had been different, I might have even enjoyed some awesome Friday nights, making memories and having some quality family time with good ol' Mom and Dad.

In reality, obedience is our *only* option. It's not like God gives us another choice. Ephesians 6:1 says, "Children, obey your parents in the Lord, for this is right" (NIV). It doesn't say, "Children, obey your parents when it's easy," or, "Children, obey your parents if you agree with them." It pretty much just says, "Obey."

This may seem so cut and dry—unreasonable almost—but we need to understand that God didn't give us these commands to make our teenage years miserable. Actually, His intent is just the opposite. God is interested in protecting us just as much or more than our parents are. He absolutely loves and adores us. We are His *children*, and He loves us as only a perfect Father can.

So, even when it's really hard and we don't understand, we have to trust God and obey Him. And even when we don't agree, if we love Him, we will keep His commandments. First John 5:3 says, "This is love for God: to obey his commands"—and one of the most important commands is that we "honor our father and mother" (NIV).

Now that I've lived a little more of life, I can see clearly how smart my parents really were. Trust me…I never thought I would say that—not in a million years. But it's true. I will probably never know the trouble they kept me out of just by saying "no." Too bad I had to give them such a hard time about it.

My Brother, My Sister—My Friend?

The old principle is sad but true: The people we love the most are often the ones we hurt the most. Unfortunately, when I was a teenager, I applied this principle to my younger sister.

In reality, I loved her very much, but I was so wrapped up in my selfish desires that, most of the time, I treated her like some sort of "subhuman." I hate to admit it, but I took my frustrations out on her—I trampled over her when I was in a bad mood, and I yelled at her for no reason at all.

I'll never forget one night two weeks before I left for college. My dad pulled me aside and said something that has stuck with me to this day. He said, "Shelley, you are going away to school in a couple of weeks, and your sister thinks that you hate her." His words cut me like a knife; I felt truly horrible.

Of course I didn't hate my sister, but once I started thinking about it, I could see that I had sure acted like I did.

Family—Shelley

I started thinking back on my relationship with Robyn. She was eight years younger than I was, so about the time I turned thirteen, she was five or six and very impressionable. A little sister naturally wants to hang out with her older sister, but I wouldn't have it!

I remember one particular weekend when Robyn, my two cousins, and I were staying at my grandparents' house while our parents were out of town. My cousins were my age, and Robyn, of course, was much younger. My cousins and I got together and chose a particularly foul-mouthed name to call Robyn—and we called her this name all weekend long. Not only did we call her names, but we wouldn't let her be a part of anything we did. It finally got to be too much for a little girl to handle, and she went off by herself to a bedroom and cried.

My cousin Bruce was touched by her tears and apologized to her and tried to console her—but not me. Now I can hardly believe how hardhearted I was. Suffice it to say, when our parents got home, we all got in big trouble for making Robyn's weekend miserable—especially me.

This was just one of many such episodes that Robyn still remembers and I still try to forget. How sad that these are the memories Robyn has of my teenage years. Such incidents were what caused my dad to speak so solemnly to me and invoke me to contemplate my actions. She and I are very close now, and although she has forgiven me, I still feel guilty over those years.

Sometimes I even find myself trying to make it up to her in some way. What I didn't realize then but what is so painfully clear to me now is that it is impossible to turn back time.

My Brother, My Sister—My Friend?

Why did I treat her so badly? I've tried to figure it out, and this is what I've come up with: Unlike people unrelated to me (like my friends), she couldn't disown me or walk away from me for good. After all, she was my sister—my own flesh and blood, so I felt I could treat her however I wanted. It just seemed like no big deal. She happened to be the closest, easiest "scapegoat." But you see, the very thing I thought justified my treating her so badly is the very thing that should have made me treat her the best of all, with the utmost love and respect. Because she is my flesh and blood, she is one of the few people who will actually remain with me throughout my whole life, one of the people I can trust the most. She—above all other friends—deserved my highest esteem. But that's not the way it went. I was just too immature to even give it a thought.

I'd venture to say that many of you are going through the very same thing—whether on the giving or receiving end. Every time we are out doing a concert and I see two siblings come through the line, I ask if they get along well. The answer is usually a strong "no!"

Why is it that we fight with our siblings like there's no tomorrow, but we're so utterly concerned about getting along with our friends? I remember walking on eggshells to avoid confrontation with my friends because I was so obsessed with their liking me, while going off on my sister without giving it a second thought.

Now, I'm sure some of you have wonderful relationships with your siblings—maybe you even consider them your best friends. You are very blessed—and very wise. But I'm also sure that many of you are like me, and with you I'd like to share two major things I'd do differently—if I had it to do over again.

1. Let your first thought be love. As a teenager, I used to listen to a Christian band called Whiteheart. One of their songs has always stuck with me. I don't remember the verses, but the chorus said, "Let your first thought, let your very first thought, be love…." Can you imagine how peacefully we could coexist with our brothers and sisters if we could train our hearts and mouths to employ this principle? When a brother or sister is nagging you or bothering you or doing something to make you mad, let your first thought be love. Now, I'll be the first to admit that this kind of response is not easy, but it is so much better than the alternative.

Ask yourself: What does love look like in this situation? A soft, sweet reply or turning the other cheek will work wonders. Or maybe you'll need to listen instead of slamming the door. Proverbs 15:1 reminds us that "a gentle answer turns away wrath, but a harsh word stirs up anger" (NIV).

When you and a brother or sister start in on each other, say a quick prayer: "Jesus, help my first thought be love, because I really do love this person." Just try it. Train yourself to take time to think and pray before you react. You won't always remember (I know, I've tried it on my husband!), but eventually God will bless your obedience, and a response of love might even become automatic and truly authentic.

2. Do something to serve your brothers and sisters at least once every day. This may seem impossible, but it doesn't have to be. It all goes back to the "Golden Rule" that you've heard all your life: "Do to others as you would have them do to you" (Matthew 7:12 NIV). I should have put it into practice with my sister.

My Brother, My Sister—My Friend?

For instance, I could have served my sister by sharing some of my "precious" time simply playing with her. I was a lot older than she and really didn't enjoy the games she liked, but fifteen minutes a day wouldn't have killed me, and it would have meant the world to her. Maybe you have an older brother. You could clean up his room or offer to clear off the table for him when it's his turn. It's little things like these that can add up to an awesome relationship.

But don't get discouraged if your siblings don't reciprocate. They have to be convicted just like you do.

Take a few minutes to contemplate your sibling relationships. Are they where they need to be? Or do they need a little work? When I was your age, no one but my parents ever suggested that I consider my relationship with my sister, and unfortunately, I didn't listen until I was leaving home. If sharing these thoughts with you can save you from the guilt and regret I felt the night my dad confronted me, I will have accomplished my purpose. Would your relationships be better if your first thought were love? Could you find ways to serve your brothers and sisters and actually treat them like friends?

Chances are, the answer is "yes."

STUDY GUIDE

Who Is Watching You?

📖 **Opening Scripture:** Begin today's study by reading 1 Timothy 4:12. Ask God to speak to you in a specific way as you study His Word.

❀ **You Are a Role Model:** Have you ever thought about the fact that you are a role model? You may not have "signed up" for that assignment, but nonetheless, you are exactly that. Although you may not know it, there is someone who looks up to you. This person watches the way you talk and the way you behave on your best and worst days. If you have a younger sibling, you can be certain he or she looks up to you. Even if you have no younger siblings, there are others who are watching. They may be neighbors, family members, or friends.

What do you think? How does that make you feel?
   ❏ Who me? I don't believe that.
   ❏ Terrified. I hope no one is watching me.
   ❏ Proud. I would be the best role model someone could follow.
   ❏ Humble. I hope I do my best to guide others in the right way.

What's your experience? What would others learn from watching your life? _____

_____

_____

_____

Who Is Watching You?

❀ Don't Let Your Youth Hurt Your Example

Fill in the blanks: Reread 1 Timothy 4:12. Fill in the missing words:
"Don't let anyone look down on you because you are _____,
but set an example for the believers in _____, in _____,
in _____, in _____ and in _____."

What do you think? Why do you think it's easy for people to look down
on those younger than they are? _____

_____

_____

What can you do to prevent others from looking down on you
because you are younger than they are?_____

_____

_____

Think about it: This verse calls us to set an example in several areas of
our lives. We are to live in such a way that we are worthy of imita-
tion. Is your life one that should be imitated by those younger than
you? Why or why not? _____

_____

_____

_____

❀ How You Can Set an Example: First Timothy 4:12 calls us to set
an example in five areas.

Family—Study Guide

1. Speech. The words that come out of our mouths have such power—to do good or harm. Consider the example you are to others in what you say.

Fill in the blanks: Read Proverbs 31:26 and fill in the missing words: "She speaks with _____, and faithful instruction is on her _____."

What's your experience? How much of the time does this statement describe you?

- ❏ Most of the time
- ❏ Are you kidding? Hardly ever.
- ❏ I try my best to grow each day.
- ❏ Every second of every day

What do you think? What are some ways you could change your words in order to be a better example? _____

_____

_____

Think about it: Are you setting an example in what you say within your family? It is easy to be careless in our words at home. We often take our families for granted and treat them worse than we do strangers. The real test of a Christian is how she speaks to her family at home.

2. Life. God has called Christians to live holy lives. It is a high calling, but it is possible when we rely on His power.

Who Is Watching You?

What does the Word say? Read Ephesians 4:1. Are there choices you need to make in order to live as He commands? If so, what are they?

_____

_____

_____

_____

3. Love. Maybe you have heard the old saying "People don't care how much you know until they know how much you care." Our love for people should set us apart as disciples of Jesus. Without it, everything else we do is just a waste of time.

What does the Word say? Read Ephesians 4:2. Why is love important in setting an example?_____

_____

_____

According to this verse, what are some actions that demonstrate our love for others? _____

_____

Think about it: Do you treat those closest to you lovingly? What about those who have harmed you? Do you model a servant heart or a "me-first" attitude? The more you grow in your relationship with Christ, the more loving you will become as God changes you from the inside out.

4. Faith. Many people claim their faith is private and not to be discussed with others. While our faith is personal, it should never stay private. Our faith should penetrate every area of life. As others watch you, do they see the difference your faith in Jesus makes? They should.

What does the Word say? Read Hebrews 11:6. What does this passage say God will do for those who earnestly seek Him?

❑ He gives them joy.
❑ He rewards them.
❑ He hides from them.
❑ He teaches them.

What do you think? What do you think it means for someone to earnestly seek Him? _____

_____

_____

How do you think God rewards those who seek Him? _____

_____

_____

Think about it: When others watch your life, can they see that you are seeking after God?

5. Purity. It doesn't take long to figure out that purity is under attack these days. It is laughed at on TV and in the movies and is considered outdated and impossible. But it is possible through God's strength.

Who Is Watching You?

What does the Word say? Read 1 Corinthians 6:18–20. According to these verses, what is your body?

❑ A work in progress

❑ Hard to control

❑ A temple of the Holy Spirit

❑ Trying to get me in constant trouble

Knowing this, how should you treat your body? _____

_____

_____

_____

Think about it: Will you commit to grow in purity? Purity is simply living according to the truth of God's Word. If so, you must guard your thoughts, your emotions, and your body.

What practical steps will you take to remain committed to purity?

_____

_____

_____

_____

_____

_____

✔ **Try This:** List one person you know who looks up to you.

_____

Family—Study Guide

Write one practical step you will take this week to be a godly role model in this person's life. _____

_____

_____

_____

_____

Remember, others will follow the footprints you leave behind. Make it your goal to lead them closer to Christ.

✝ **Living the Word:** Read Luke 17:1–2.

• What does Jesus say about those who cause others to sin? _____

_____

_____

• To whom do you think the passage is referring when it speaks of "little ones"? _____

_____

_____

_____

• What are some ways we cause others to sin? _____

_____

_____

_____

_____

Who Is Watching You?

• How are you careful to avoid setting a bad example? _____

_____

_____

• Your influence can be used for good or bad. Will you choose to
leave a legacy of holiness? _____

Dear Point Of Grace,

I think my parents are getting a divorce. They fight almost every night, and they say the most horrible things to each other. I hate it when they yell. I just stay in my room and pray that they will be nice to each other.

The other night they were fighting because I wanted some money for new jeans to wear to a party. First they fought about how much money I was allowed to spend on clothes, and then they fought about whether or not I should be allowed to go to the party. Hearing them fight makes me feel like it's all my fault.

I can't stand the thought of not having one of them in my home. It feels like it's me that's splitting up, not them. Why doesn't God answer my prayers to keep them together, or does He even care about things like this?

Julie

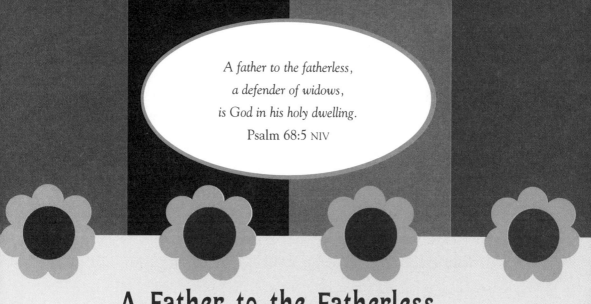

A father to the fatherless,
a defender of widows,
is God in his holy dwelling.
Psalm 68:5 NIV

A Father to the Fatherless

I know I'm stating the obvious, but not all families are happy. Not every family is made up of Mom, Dad, two kids, and a dog. Not every home is a safe, secure place to be. Some of you are dealing with the pain of divorce or abandonment by a parent. Some of you live with non-Christian parents or simply feel unloved. Others of you may be in situations of serious abuse (emotional or physical) and really need help beyond this book. (I'll talk a little about that later.) If you're struggling with any of these situations or feelings, this devotional is for you.

Because I came from such a good home, at first I felt intimidated about even approaching this subject. But as I thought about it, I realized that God and His Word supply us with some basic truths that are helpful no matter who the "messenger" (me) is.

1. God cares. The first truth I want to share is that God cares! First Peter 5:7 says it so beautifully: "Cast all your anxiety on him because he cares for you" (NIV). God knows all about you and your heartaches. He even knows how many hairs are on your head. Luke 12:6–7 explains our value to God this way: "Are not five sparrows sold for two pennies? Yet not one of them is forgotten by God. Indeed, the very hairs of your head are all numbered. Don't be afraid; you are worth more than many sparrows" (NIV). God cares for you.

2. Jesus understands. Imagine if you had a friend who *always* understood what you were going through. I mean, *really* understood—even had been through it herself. And when you talked to her, she was all ears, comforting you, never saying "Let me call you back" or "I can't help you with this one. It's too messy." Imagine a person who was so consistent in her friendship that she seemed perfect. Sound impossible? It is! No earthly friend could be that good, but Jesus can. Jesus is a friend who really understands.

In fact, Hebrews 4:15 says this about Jesus, our High Priest: "This High Priest of ours understands our weaknesses, for he faced all of the same temptations we do, yet he did not sin" (NLT). Do you get that? He sympathizes with us, and He understands how we feel. He understands how it feels to be betrayed, lonely, and mistreated. He understands because He has been there.

3. God works all things together for good. Even though God cares very much for us, bad things still happen. I don't know all the answers to why God allows our parents to divorce, our dads to walk out, abuse to take place, or innocent children to suffer for things that are totally out of their control. I do know that Satan has *some* power in this world, and I know that all the evil in this world originates with him.

But God has *ultimate* power. Though Satan brings pain and suffering into this world, God will ultimately bring good. One of my very favorite promises in the Bible is in Romans 8:28: "We know that all things work together for good to those who love God, and to those who are the called according to His purpose" (NKJV). This verse doesn't say that only good things will happen to you. It says that God will work everything *together* for good.

There will be times in your life when you experience pain you never thought possible. There will be times when bad things happen to you. At those times, you must reach out and claim the promise of Romans 8:28. You must believe that God is weaving all the circumstances of your life into a gorgeous tapestry. On the backside, you can see mistakes and backstitches and ugly knots, but on the front, you see a beautiful arrangement of color and design.

4. Fervent prayer is effective. Our friend Jesus will help us through any and every thing that life sends our way, but we need to *ask* for that help through prayer. When our world throws us problems that we didn't sign up for, we need to throw ourselves on Him.

Jesus wants us to talk to Him about our problems, and this applies to problems at home. But we must come to Him in fervent prayer. *Fervent* means "extremely passionate enthusiasm." James 5:16 says that "the effective, fervent prayer of a righteous man avails much" (NKJV).

Fervent prayer is *not* just throwing up a quick, mindless prayer and expecting our problems to vanish. Fervent prayer means taking the time to really pour our hearts out to God with an attitude of submission to Him and a willingness to learn what *we* can do to make a difference. Fervent prayer takes real energy and can even be hard work.

I've discovered that it's only when I pray fervently and wholeheartedly—with everything in me—that I sense His true presence and comfort and an overall feeling that everything is going to be OK.

5. God is a father to the fatherless. Psalm 68:5–6 says that God is a "father to the fatherless" and a "defender of widows." What a beautiful picture of a loving God. It goes on to say that He "places the lonely in families" and "sets the prisoners free and gives them joy" (NLT). Isn't that what we want when we feel lonely—to be part of a family, to belong? And have you ever felt like a prisoner in your home circumstances? This verse says that God sets prisoners free and gives them joy.

There are other places in the Bible that talk about God's special love and care for the fatherless: Deuteronomy 10:18 says, "He defends the cause of the fatherless and the widow" (NIV), and 24:17 says, "Do not deprive the alien or the fatherless of justice" (NIV). Proverbs 23:10–11 warns, "Do not move an ancient boundary stone or encroach on the fields of the fatherless, for their Defender is strong; he will take up their case against you" (NIV). Psalm 27:10 says, "Even if my father and mother abandon me, the LORD will hold me close" (NLT).

Do you get the feeling that God has a special place in His heart for those who are without a father or mother? Can't you hear His compassion and protection ringing loudly from those scriptures?

A Father to the Fatherless

It's just my opinion, but I've always thought that God has something extraspecial in mind for those who don't have an earthly father, that He will show Himself to them in an awesome way reserved only for them.

6. Obey even non-Christian parents. I often hear the question "Do I still have to obey my parents if they're not Christians?" The answer is *yes*—absolutely. God calls us to be loving, obedient children whether or not our parents are believers. The ultimate goal is that through prayer and our example that they, too, will come to Christ. This is unlikely if your example as a Christian includes disobedience.

Now, there is an exception to this. In extreme circumstances, children are sometimes asked to do things that are wrong or that use their bodies in a way not intended by God. If this is happening to you, you must tell someone immediately and get some help. Go to an adult friend you trust—a pastor, a teacher, or a parent of a friend. But tell someone. Mercy Ministries of America (1-800-922-9131) is a group that can direct you to someone in your area who can help you, and your call to them will be completely confidential.

7. Your parents' problems are not your fault. It's important that you understand that you have absolutely no control over what happens between your mom and dad. You don't have the power to make them stay married or the power to pull them apart. You only have control over how *you* deal with the broken pieces. As unfair as that sounds, that's how life is. We don't get to pick and choose what comes our way, but we do get to choose how we respond.

God designed families as a place for people to grow and learn about love, sharing, sacrifice, and much more. He also designed families to provide love and security to all their members. And when families don't work as God intended, pain results. God knows this and is ready to comfort us.

Maybe your parents are divorced, and you don't have a mom or dad who is there for you. Maybe you've never even known your father or mother. Or maybe your parents are both in your home, but they aren't Christians, and this makes you feel alone.

Whatever your circumstances, God is on your side. He is for you. He is closer than you think. Satan would love nothing more than to use the problems in your family to thwart your relationship with God. *Don't let him do it!*

With God's help, you can turn your circumstances around for good and become more like Jesus in the process. How can living through your parents' divorce make you more like Jesus? I believe that pain can make you stronger in character, more sympathetic to others with similar problems, and, most important, more dependent on God—who is the best and most perfect parent we could ever want.

Along life's road
There will be sunshine and rain,
Roses and thorns, laughter and pain.
And 'cross the miles
You will face mountains so steep,
Deserts so long,
and valleys so deep.
Sometimes the journey's gentle,
Sometimes the cold winds blow,
But I want you to remember,
I want you to know—

You will never walk alone

you will never walk alone

Making the Best of Your Situation

📖 **Opening Scripture:** Pray that God would speak to you in a specific way today as you study His Word. Read Philippians 4:12.

❧ **The Secret of Contentment:** Not every home is an ideal one, and many things in your home are not under your control. You can't fix other people. But you can learn to be content in whatever situation you find yourself.

Fill in the blanks: Reread Philippians 4:12 and fill in the missing words: "I know what it is to be in _____, and I know what it is to have _____. I have learned the _____ of being _____ in any and every _____."

What's your experience? What about your family life is not ideal? _____

_____

_____

Have you learned any "secrets" about being content in your situation? Write them here: _____

_____

_____

Pray about it: Commit to praying for each member of your family. As you do this, you will begin to see them through Jesus' eyes. Prayer changes our focus from the present to eternity and helps us be more content.

If any of your family members don't know Christ, ask God to draw them to Himself. Pray that they will become aware of their need for salvation.

Think about it: Prayer breeds thankfulness in our hearts, and thankfulness breeds contentment. Read Philippians 1:3–4. How can praying for those in your family help you be more content with them?

❧ **Acknowledge Every Day as a Gift from God:** A person who makes the best of her situation uses the opportunities God places in front of her. She acknowledges that each day is a gift from God. She unwraps it carefully and honors Him in the way she treats this gift.

Fill in the blanks: Psalm 118:24: "This is the _____ the Lord has made; let us _____ and be _____ in it."

Think about it: What things about your family can you rejoice and be glad about? _____
_____

❧ **Living for a Higher Purpose:** As we learn to make the best of our situations, we must sometimes relinquish the right to live for our own will and satisfaction and live for a higher purpose—serving others.

Family—Study Guide

Fill in the blanks: Read Matthew 10:39. Fill in the missing words:
"Whoever _____ his life will lose it, and whoever loses his life
for my sake _____."

Think about it: This verse is not talking about literal life and death.
Instead, it refers to the goals and motives we have for our lives.
When we live for our own satisfaction and happiness, we will only
become emptier. On the other hand, when we seek to please our
Master first, we will find purpose and freedom.

What's your experience? Have you ever sacrificed your own happiness to
serve another and found joy in the process? If so, describe that experience. _____

_____

✣ **Learning to Get Along:** Read Philippians 2:1–4. What do you
think verse 2 means when it calls us to be "like-minded"?

❑ Totally alike in every belief and idea
❑ Striving toward unity with others in the body of Christ
❑ Open-minded
❑ Focused on the truth of God's Word

What do you think? What are some practical ways you can become
more like-minded with others in your family even though you may
not agree with them 100 percent of the time? _____

_____

_____

_____

❧ Putting Others First

Fill in the blanks: Reread Philippians 2:3. Fill in the missing words: "Do _____ out of selfish ambition or vain conceit, but in _____ consider others _____ than yourselves."

Think about it: Ouch! This verse may seem impossible, but when we rely on God's power, we find the strength necessary to obey. Followers of Jesus put others first. They seek to live this way every day. Of course they aren't perfect, but when they mess up, they ask for forgiveness and move on.

What do you think? What is the most challenging thing about putting others first? _____

_____

_____

_____

What's your experience? Do you know someone who consistently puts others first? If so, describe the impact that person has on those around them. _____

_____

_____

_____

Family—Study Guide

Think about it: You will not have your family forever. Someday you will no longer share a home with them. Will you commit to serve your family while you have the chance? If so, begin today.

How often do you serve the people in your family?

❏ I do this all the time.

❏ I do this often, but I could do it even more.

❏ I can't remember the last time I did this.

❏ I rarely do this, but I want to change.

Philippians 2:4 says to look to others' interests. Make a list of the people in your family. Next to each name write down this person's interests and concerns. List some practical actions you can take to support this person. _____

_____

_____

_____

✔ **Try This:** Find a picture of your entire family. It might be a picture from last Christmas or one from a recent vacation.

Take a few moments to really look at the faces in that picture. What do you see? Do you see those with whom you constantly fight? Do you see those who have hurt you?

Take some time to prayerfully look at that picture and ask God to give you His perspective about the members of your family. Did you know that He loves each one dearly? He sent His Son to die for every person in that picture. Will you choose to allow God's perspective to influence the way you treat the people in that picture?

Place this picture somewhere so you will see it each day. You may even want to put it in your Bible. Will you commit to daily pray for the people in this picture? If so, sign your name in the space provided.

_____

✝ **Living the Word:** Read Philippians 2:5–8.
• Describe the attitude of Jesus Christ as shown in these verses.

_____

_____

_____

• In what ways can you choose to have the same attitude in your daily life? _____

_____

_____

• Is there something specific you can do today to adopt the role of a servant in your family? If so, what is it? _____

_____

_____

_____

_____

beauty tips

✿ To prevent lipstick from fading, apply foundation to lips, then blot. Apply lip liner and blot. Apply lipstick and blot again.

✿ When applying blush, less is more. Look in the mirror and smile widely to find the apple of the cheek. With short, light strokes apply blush to the apple.

✿ To shape nails, choose the shape best for your nails. If you have an oval-shaped cuticle at the base, the square look works well. If your cuticles are pointed, an oval shaped nail looks best.

✿ Curling your eyelashes helps open up the face. Even if you don't use much makeup, this can be a very useful tool.

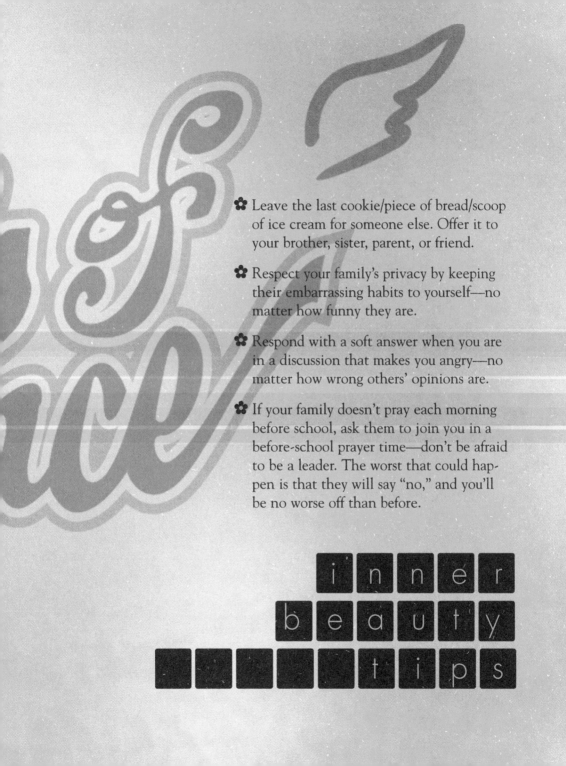

❁ Leave the last cookie/piece of bread/scoop of ice cream for someone else. Offer it to your brother, sister, parent, or friend.

❁ Respect your family's privacy by keeping their embarrassing habits to yourself—no matter how funny they are.

❁ Respond with a soft answer when you are in a discussion that makes you angry—no matter how wrong others' opinions are.

❁ If your family doesn't pray each morning before school, ask them to join you in a before-school prayer time—don't be afraid to be a leader. The worst that could happen is that they will say "no," and you'll be no worse off than before.

inner
beauty
tips

Terry

friends

Dear Point Of Grace,

I feel like no one cares about me. I mean, I'm pretty sure it's not true, but it's still the way I feel. It even seems that my best friend doesn't care about me! I'm not the type of person who shares my feelings with others. This has been a problem for me. I'm afraid to let anyone get close to me. I'm afraid of getting hurt.

I know God is always right beside me and that He is my closest friend, but I still feel lonely and sad. I want to make new friends, but I don't even know what kind of friend to look for. Can you help me?

April

A friend loves at all times,
and a brother is born for adversity.
Proverbs 17:17 NIV

What a Friend Is

What is a friend? There are probably as many definitions of *friend* as there are girls reading this book. *The Student Bible* says that friends know, like, and trust one another; they support and sympathize with each other. Isn't that what we all want in a friend? Someone who knows us and likes us anyway. Someone we can trust with our most secret secrets; someone who'll support us when we feel like we're falling apart; someone who'll feel our pain with us.

When I look back on my life, some of my very best memories are times spent with friends. Just thinking about them makes me smile and brings warmth to my heart. Friends have given me laughter in my tears, joy in my sorrow, and unconditional love when I felt completely unlovable. It's not how *many* friends we have that matters, but the precious *qualities* of those friends. Listen to what the Bible says in Proverbs 18:24 (I've paraphrased it just a little): "A girl of many friends may come to ruin, but a really good friend sticks closer than a sister." What this means is that you need a couple of close friends with whom you can share your real self, rather than many friends who won't stick with you through thick and thin.

When I think about the friends who've meant the most to me throughout my life, I see several characteristics that make them my "true" friends. Let's look at what it takes to make a real friend. A good friend is:

1. Loyal and Trustworthy. Hear me when I say: A good friend does not talk harmfully about a friend behind her back. I have felt the pain of this in my own life. It may seem innocent and even fun, but it will kill a friendship fast. Real friends do not tell each others' secrets. A real friend is someone to whom you can tell *anything*—even something that would make great "gossip"—without fear that she will betray your trust.

You may think it's impossible to be a truly faithful friend at this stage in your life, but it's not. "A gossip goes around revealing secrets, but those who are trustworthy can keep a confidence" (Proverbs 11:13 NLT).

2. Honest. Being honest with our friends isn't always easy, but it is so important. If we let hurt feelings and misunderstandings go unresolved, they will fester in our hearts, and bitterness and distrust will take root. I am very honest with my friends—sometimes maybe even a little too blunt. But it is this honesty that has allowed us to remain friends. I tell my friends when they hurt me, and they tell me when I hurt them. I can count on them to call me out on a wrong. We hold each other accountable. Proverbs 27:5–6 says, "An open rebuke is better than hidden love! Wounds from a friend are better than many kisses from an enemy" (NLT).

What a Friend Is

In learning how to be honest but kind, a good place to start is Ephesians 4:15. It tells us to *speak the truth in love*. This simple rule will help you know when and how to tell a possibly painful truth. Honesty doesn't mean spouting off out of anger or just to get things "off our chest." Truth must always be tempered by love.

3. Forgiving. Unconditional forgiveness is key to any relationship. In marriage you have to forgive even when you think you're right or have been hurt. Consider friendship a practice for your future marriage. Ephesians 4:32 says, "Be kind to each other, tenderhearted, forgiving one another, just as God through Christ has forgiven you" (NLT). We all mess up—often! None of us likes to admit our imperfections, but being aware of our weaknesses helps us to be forgiving of the imperfections in others. If we expect our friendships to last, we must forgive and ask for forgiveness. Even the most hurtful things can be forgiven and put to rest.

4. Spiritually Encouraging and Supportive. Kind words from my closest friends help my self-esteem and encourage me spiritually more than almost anything else. You can encourage your friends by little things you say and do. Tell your friends how sweet, caring, and precious they are. Tell them how cute they look or that you love a new outfit. Focus on your friends' inner qualities, too—like their kindness or great attitude in a difficult time.

Seek out friends who share your Christian beliefs. If we don't hang out with spiritually uplifting friends, we will drown in our walk with God. You cannot be a godly girl all alone. Hebrews 3:13 talks about encouraging each other: "Encourage one another daily, as long as it is still called Today, so that none of you may be hardened by sin's deceitfulness" (NIV). When Jesus is the foundation of a friendship, it will go much deeper than any other friendship.

There's a special kind of encouragement called "accountability." This means that you "answer" to a friend for how you behave on a date or how you're doing in your relationship with God. When you're accountable to someone, you are obligated, in a sense, to share openly with her about how things *really* are with you—and she shares how things are with her. I encourage you to choose someone in your life—someone who is trustworthy—to be your accountability partner. If you'll do this, you'll be challenged to grow in ways you may never be able to grow alone.

5. A Good Listener. If all we do is talk, not many people will want to be around us. A true friend is skilled in the art of listening. When our friends share problems with us, our first instinct is to try to "fix" things. But sometimes the very best thing we can do is be quiet and just listen. I struggle with this one because advice just seems to flow out of my mouth. Most of the time, what is really needed is my attentive heart and my prayers. "Do you see a [girl] who speaks in haste? There is more hope for a fool than for [her]" (Proverbs 29:20 NIV). James 1:19 says, "Be quick to listen, slow to speak" (NIV). My best advice on this topic is that you should pray and not talk. If a friend asks for your advice, be wise in giving your opinion. If the problem is a serious one, you might need to direct your friend to your youth minister or pastor.

6. Someone You Can Be Yourself with—All the Time. There is no greater joy than feeling free enough to completely let your guard down with a friend. My husband, Chris, and a small group of girlfriends are the only people I really do that with. I am not saying I'm not myself around other people, but when I'm with these people, I know they will love me no matter how I am. When I know I am not being judged, I know I am with a friend. I've heard it said that "True friends are the ones who really know you but love you anyway." I like that.

7. Available. Imagine having a "friend" who announced that she was available only on Fridays and Tuesday mornings. You would think she was crazy. It's not fun to ask someone to do things with you and always get turned down. I have friends whom I can call at any hour of the day or night and know that they will be instantly available to me. Of course, we can't abuse this aspect of friendship and demand all of our friends' time, but real friends are available to each other and care about each others' needs. "Each of you should look not only to your own interests, but also to the interests of others" (Philippians 2:4 NIV). Being interested in and available to your friends will shape you into a "best" friend.

8. Giving and Helpful. "God loves a cheerful giver" (2 Corinthians 9:7 NIV). When a friend is in trouble, don't annoy her by asking what you can do; fig-ure out something helpful and do it. When you were a baby, you were natu-rally selfish. You were helpless and demanded that others do everything for you. But now you are at a time in your life when you need to be unselfish. It's time to look at a friend and see what she needs rather than focusing on what you need from her. Learn the art of giving unselfishly, and you will truly be happy.

9. Godly. When you hang out with the wrong people, you will have more problems than the friendships are worth. Trust me on this: Don't get caught up with people who are bad influences. "Do not be misled: 'Bad company corrupts good character'" (1 Corinthians 15:33 NIV). Friendship with such people will only be temporary, and the wrong kinds of friends can bring you great heartbreak. You know when someone is a bad influence. Use your head to be strong and wise. "Be careful how you live, not as fools but as those who are wise" (Ephesians 5:15 NLT). "Fear the LORD and shun evil" (Proverbs 3:7 NIV). Search out friends who share your belief in God. We don't want to shun people, but we must be wise in who we allow to influence us.

10. Someone Who Laughs with You. Laughter is medicine to your soul. The wise King Solomon tells us in Ecclesiates 3:1 and 4 that "There is a time for everything, and a season for every activity under heaven...a time to weep and a time to laugh, a time to mourn and a time to dance" (NIV). Friends are people we share good times with. We connect with them through tears and through laughter. Ethel Barrymore said that "you grow up the day you have the first real laugh at yourself." How true. People who are sure enough of themselves to laugh at their shortcomings are relaxing to be with. Laughter reminds us not to take life too seriously. I love the feeling of laughing when I feel like falling apart. It releases stress to have a good laugh with friends.

Now that you know what a true friend is made of, you know what to look for in others, and you know what to strive for in your own life.

If you weep,
I will weep with you.
If you sing for joy,
the rest of us
will lift our voices too.
But no matter what you
feel inside,
there's no need to pretend—
**That's the way it is in this
circle of friends.**

circle of friends

STUDY GUIDE

Friends to Encourage Me

📖 **Opening Scripture:** Ask God to speak to you in a specific way as you study His Word. Then read Proverbs 13:20.

❧ **"Identical" Friends:** Has anyone ever seen you with your best friend and pointed out how alike the two of you are? Maybe they noticed that you wear your hair the same way, talk alike, or have the same sense of humor. Good friends often tend to share the same tastes, interests, and dreams. Why is this so? Friends "rub off" on each other. They influence each other in ways that are obvious and in others that aren't quite as easy to see.

What's your experience? List one way that you and a good friend are alike. _____

❧ **The Power of a Friend's Influence:** Friends can influence us for the better, as well as for the worse. Sometimes they bring out the best in us and challenge us to grow.

What's your experience? Describe one instance when a friend influenced you for the better. _____

At other times friends can cause us to compromise our standards and lose sight of what is best for our lives. Describe a time when a friend's influence caused you to behave in a way you later regretted.

Friends to Encourage Me

_____

_____

❖ Walk with the Wise

What does the Word say? Reread Proverbs 13:20. What do you think this verse means by "walking with the wise"?

❏ Running a marathon next to someone extremely intelligent

❏ Carefully selecting friends who live according to biblical standards

❏ Never associating with people who are non-Christians

❏ Always keeping our eyes and ears open to see what is around us

When the Bible speaks of "walking with" someone, it refers to allowing that person close access into our lives. It means the more time we spend with people, the more they will influence us.

What's your experience? Which of your friends has the greatest influence on you? _____

Think about it: Do you walk with the wise? Do your friends encourage you to follow Christ and become more like Him? If so, you will find that the more time you spend with them, the more you will grow in your relationship with Christ. On the other hand, if your friends constantly laugh at your faith or tempt you to compromise, the more time you spend with them, the more you will drift in your commitment to Christ.

Friends—Study Guide

✿ Unwise Relationships

Fill in the blanks: Fill in the missing words from Proverbs 13:20: "A _____ of fools suffers_____."

What do you think? In what ways could you suffer harm by being friends with those who are foolish? _____

_____

_____

_____

Pray about it: In reading this, you may have realized you have some friends who are causing you harm. If so, you probably need to limit the time you spend with them. Ask God to help you replace unhealthy friendships with friends who encourage you in your walk with Him. This doesn't mean you never speak to your old friends again; it just means you reduce the influence they have over you.

You may want to make different choices about the activities you participate in with them. Start praying for God to soften their hearts to His love. Take opportunities He gives you to share with them. You can still be involved in their lives, but your closest friends should be those who encourage you to walk with Him.

✿ Friendly Encouragement:
Read Hebrews 3:12–13. The word *encouragement* literally means "to breathe courage into another."

What's your experience? List some people you know who encourage you in your walk with Christ. _____

Friends to Encourage Me

_____

_____

What do you think? In what ways can you follow the command in this verse to "encourage one another daily"? _____

_____

What warning do you find in the passage? _____

_____

What's your experience? How can encouragement keep us from becoming "hardened by sin's deceitfulness"? _____

_____

_____

_____

_____

❖ **Enjoy Being Part of a Church Family:** God never intended for us to walk the journey of faith alone. He provides Christian friends, mentors, and leaders to help us as we seek to become more like Christ. His will is for you to be involved in a local church where you learn about His Word and live in unity with other Christians.

What does the Word say? Read Hebrews 10:24–25. Why is it so important that Christians don't give up meeting with each other? _____

_____

_____

Friends—Study Guide

❧ **Meet with an Accountability Group:** In addition to participating in a church that teaches God's Word, you may also consider meeting together with a group of friends for the purpose of spiritual growth. Girls will use any excuse to get together, right? Well, why not ask some friends to form an accountability group with you?

An ideal group consists of anywhere from three to six girls who also want to grow in their relationships with Christ. You might decide to meet once a week to discuss what God is teaching each of you. You can also share struggles and areas where you need to grow. Accountability partners pray with and for each other. They keep a high level of trust, knowing that the things shared in confidence will be treated with discretion.

What's your experience? Read James 5:16. How vulnerable can you be with your Christian friends about your personal struggles?

- ❏ I feel like I must constantly put on an act that I am doing OK.
- ❏ My friends don't have the time to listen to my silly problems.
- ❏ If I opened up to my friends, they would pray for me and support me.
- ❏ I don't have a Christian friend whom I could go to about a problem.

Pray about it: Christian friends make all the difference during the hard times in life. They point us to Christ and support us by praying for us. If you do not have friends like this, start praying for some today.

Friends to Encourage Me

✔ **Try This:** Write down the names of three people you know who may be interested in forming an accountability group. Ask them this week to pray about whether they would like to be involved. If you do not know anyone right now whom you think would be interested, pray and wait. God will faithfully bring the right people in the right time. _____

✟ **Living the Word:** Read Proverbs 27:17.

• Just as iron is sharpened by constant friction rubbing against it, we are challenged as we allow our lives to be closely connected with other Christians. How has God used someone else to make you "sharper"?

• We must be vulnerable in order to have our lives challenged by others. How easy is it for you to be honest about your needs and shortcomings? _____

• What practical steps can you take that will assure you will be sharpened by other Christians? _____

_____

_____

Dear Point Of Grace,

How am I supposed to find a real friend when most of the girls I've been friends with have stabbed me in the back? Sometimes girls can be so evil to each other. How can I find a true friend?

It seems like the people I get along with best are the people who end up getting me into trouble. How do I know what kind of friends to choose?

Erin

Don't think only about your own affairs, but be interested in others, too, and what they are doing.

Philippians 2:4 NLT

What a Friend Isn't

In my last devotional, we talked about what a true friend is. Now we need to talk about what a friend isn't. The way I see it, the five biggest problem areas in teenage friendships are gossip, criticism, cliques, jealousy, and trying to please others so much that you sacrifice what is right. Let's see what the Bible says about these areas and shed some light on areas you may need to work on.

Gossip. OK. Let's be honest. We all gossip to some extent. Some of it may seem harmless, but I'll bet you've had some experiences where it was very harmful—whether you were the one being gossiped about or the one doing the gossiping. And while we're being honest, let's just go ahead and admit that we sometimes gossip about others to gain popularity or to make ourselves look good. And the truth is, sharing a juicy piece of gossip sometimes gets you on the "inside," but only for a moment.

There are two kinds of gossip: telling a lie about someone and telling something that was told to you in confidence. Both of these will ruin a friendship faster than anything else. Proverbs 16:28 says that "gossip separates the best of friends" (NLT). Now, think about it: If your friend gossips about other people, why wouldn't she gossip about you? If she constantly talks bad about others when they aren't around, what makes you think she doesn't talk about you when you're not around? If you can't trust a friend, why continue the relationship? Let's turn this around for a minute: If others can't trust *you*, why should they want to be *your* friend?

The damage that gossip does is hard to repair. "It's harder to make amends with an offended friend than to capture a fortified city. Arguments separate friends like a gate locked with iron bars" (Proverbs 18:19 NLT). That is a pretty heavy verse. A fortified city and iron bars cannot be easily broken into—that is how hard it would be to restore a friendship after gossip has separated it.

The power of our words is almost frightening. "The tongue is a small thing, but what enormous damage it can do. A tiny spark can set a great forest on fire. And the tongue is a flame of fire. It is full of wickedness that can ruin your whole life" (James 3:5–6 NLT). If we can learn to keep our fiery tongues under control, we can gain a reputation as a trustworthy person. Proverbs 11:13 says, "Those who are trustworthy can keep a confidence" (NLT). But if we don't control our tongues, the Bible also tells us in Proverbs 25:10 that we will have a hard time regaining our reputation once we are pegged as a gossip.

Don't gossip; don't even listen to gossip. Defend your friends, and they will defend you.

Criticism. OK, we're probably all feeling a bit guilty right now, so let's move on to criticism. This, like gossip, can seem harmless, but it cuts like a knife. Sometimes what we mean as an "innocent" joke can really hurt. Maybe we're just goofing around when we tell a friend, "You're so stupid," but our words can throw daggers into the hearts of others. Most people are hurt by that kind of joking, but some don't show it. They don't want to give you another reason to criticize them. Do you joke too much?

All of us are insecure at times. So work at being sensitive to the feelings of others, even if it is not natural for you. Use self-control in your choice of words. Stop and think before you blurt out your thoughts. Think about how you would feel if someone said to you what you say to them. Negative criticism may sometimes seem fun, but others will learn not to trust you if you are constantly critical. Be encouraging, and you will be trusted and well liked.

Let this prayer from God's Word be in your heart always: "May the words of my mouth and the thoughts of my heart be pleasing to you, O LORD, my rock and my redeemer" (Psalm 19:14 NLT).

Cliques. Webster's dictionary defines a *clique* as "a narrow, exclusive circle or group of persons; especially one held together by common interests, views, or purposes." Now, according to that definition, cliques aren't all bad. We can find security and acceptance in a group of people who share our interests and purposes. I still remember my high-school days and how glad I was to belong to a group as I went to awkward dances and football games. But what makes a clique bad is when it is exclusive—and this happens a lot at school and, yes, even at church. Cliques are often made up of the "popular" kids, and they exclude people who aren't pretty enough or popular enough.

Friends—Terry

I remember seeing the cliques at my high school and wanting to be popular, too. I think it is natural to want to be liked. Thankfully, though, I didn't hang out with the most popular "in crowd." I saved myself a lot of heartache by not striving to be popular and by just being myself. I hung out with the choir and a few handpicked buddies who loved me for me and not because of how I looked or how talented I was. I also did a lot with our youth group, and it was a wonderful blend of all different kinds of neat Christian kids. They accepted me, and I accepted them. What was great about that group was that what held us together was Jesus.

Being a follower of Jesus often means doing things the hard way. It means befriending those who are left out of all the other groups—it means being kind to the unlovable. These people don't have to be your closest friends, but Jesus tells us that loving those who love us is really no big deal. He asks us to love those who don't love us: "If you love those who love you, what credit is that to you? For even 'sinners' love those who love them. And if you do good to those who do good to you, what credit is that to you? For even 'sinners' do that" (Luke 6:32–33 NIV). We are called to love people who are hard to love, not just the popular kids.

I was the kid nobody knew when I was a ninth-grader in a new school in Oklahoma. But there was a girl there who reached out to me and became one of my best friends. She later became my maid of honor, and she and I are still close friends today. Marti and I had some classes together, and she noticed that I was alone. She started by asking me to eat lunch with her. She got me involved in choir simply by inviting me and assuring me that I would like it. Simple efforts, but they made the world of difference to me.

Her kindness inspired me to do the same for others at school and church. I hope some of them remember me with the same fondness and appreciation that I have for Marti. You, too, can be remembered as the person who befriended someone who was alone—even though he or she wasn't popular or pretty or whatever.

Look at your own situation. Do you have a group you hang out with? Did you choose your group because they can make you look good? Do you exclude those who aren't quite cool enough? The words of the apostle Paul in the Book of Philippians give us some serious guidelines to consider when it comes to the people we hang out with: "Don't be selfish; don't live to make a good impression on others. Be humble, thinking of others as better than yourself. Don't think only about your own affairs, but be interested in others, too, and what they are doing" (2:3–4 NLT).

True friends don't look for what they can get out of other people or how good other people make them look. True friends see others through the eyes of God.

Jealousy. Another thing I see us girls struggle with is jealousy. We want what someone else has. It is so easy for us to see the good things about someone else and not recognize our own qualities.

We are jealous of superficial things like clothes, hair, body types, and money; but we are also jealous of people who have a lot of friends or a great personality. Jealousy is a poison that can eat away at the good inside of you until it eventually overcomes your thoughts. Proverbs 14:30 says, "A heart at peace gives life to the body, but envy rots the bones" (NIV).

You can't control everything in your life, but you can control whether or not you allow jealousy into your heart. One of the best ways to get jealousy out of your heart is to replace it with memorized Scriptures like James 3:16–17: "Wherever there is jealousy and selfish ambition, there you will find disorder and every kind of evil. But the wisdom that comes from heaven is first of all pure. It is also peace loving, gentle at all times, and willing to yield to others. It is full of mercy and good deeds. It shows no partiality and is always sincere" (NLT).

Another great way to keep jealousy out of your heart is to be concerned for and help others. Jealousy and selfishness often go hand in hand. I ask you to look outside your own life for a bit. Ask what you can do for others, take the focus off yourself, and your jealousy will dwindle. Fill your mind with helping others and think on good things. Philippians 4:8 tells us, "Whatever is true, whatever is noble, whatever is right, whatever is pure, whatever is lovely, whatever is admirable—if anything is excellent or praiseworthy—think about such things" (NIV).

Be content with what you have, set goals that build on what God has given you, and focus on giving more than getting. Try to be happy for people when they do or receive something good, and you will be happier yourself.

Trying to Please Others. Finally, a friend is not someone who puts pressure on you to do something you know is wrong. Some people call this peer pressure; I call it trying too hard to please others. The Bible is our best source for knowing what is right and wrong. Beyond that, most of us have a basic instinct—a conscience—that tells us what's right and what's wrong. Use your head, and don't give in to pressure. Doing what you know is wrong will come back to haunt you in the end.

Not long ago, I received a letter from a girl asking if she should go to clubs with her non-Christian friends to better her relationships with them. Well, you don't have to think long to figure out that she should not be hanging around clubs for any reason. And she may need to reconsider how close she gets to those friends. There's a fine line between being exclusive and snobby in your Christianity and hanging around people who pull you down. As I quoted in the first devotional, 1 Corinthians 15:33 tells us plainly that "bad company corrupts good morals" (NASB). And 1 Corinthians 6:18 tells us to "flee immorality" (NASB). That means *run away from it!*

Be loving and kind to all people, but be careful about choosing the people you spend a lot of time with. Your closest friends should be those who encourage you to do right, not pressure you to do wrong.

Think about the kind of friend you are and examine the people you hang out with. Do you or your friends gossip about others? Are you critical of other people? Are you part of a group that excludes others? Do your friends put pressure on you to do what is wrong?

Pray for good friendships, and God will bring them to you. Just be patient. Good friends are some of the most precious treasures we can have; but bad friends are worse than no friends, and worst of all, they can pull you away from your best friend—Jesus.

Me and My Big Mouth

📖 **Opening Scripture:** Read Psalm 19:14. Ask God to speak to you in a specific way as you study His Word today.

❧ **What's the Big Deal about Words?** Have you ever noticed that when girlfriends get together, the words are fast and many? It seems that we just speak the first things that come into our minds without taking time to think. How many times have you said something only to feel the "pang" of conviction later? It is good to have friends we feel comfortable with, but we must remember that familiarity doesn't give us the license to sin.

What's your experience? Has there ever been a time when you said something you later regretted? If so, how did you feel when you realized your mistake? _____

What were the consequences that you or someone else suffered?_____

_____

_____

❧ **Tongue Control**

What does the Word say? Read James 3:2. What does this passage say about someone who is never at fault in what he says?

    ❑ He is an angel.

    ❑ He has a bad case of laryngitis.

Me and My Big Mouth

❏ He must be a preacher.

❏ He is able to keep his whole body in check.

Think about it: This passage teaches that those who can control their mouths are able to control other areas of their lives. On the other hand, those who never learn to control their words will find they don't practice self-control in other areas.

What do you think? Why do you think we have such a hard time controlling the words we speak?

❏ Our mouths have minds of their own.

❏ We lack self-control.

❏ We talk in our sleep.

❏ We are afraid of staying silent.

What's your experience? Do you know someone who uses self-control in the way they speak to and about others? If so, describe what it is like to be around this person. _____

_____

_____

_____

❧ The Small Controls the Mighty

Fill in the blanks: Read James 3:3–12. Fill in the blanks from James 3:3: "When we put_____ into the mouths of horses to make them obey us, we can turn the _____ animal."

James 3:4: "Or take ships as an example. Although they are so large and are driven by strong winds, they are steered by a _____ _____ _____ wherever the pilot wants to go."

Think about it: Although the tongue is such a small and hidden part of the body, it can control the whole individual. It is compared to a bit that steers a horse or a rudder that directs a ship. The tongue, although it is a very small part of the body, will chart the course of your life.

What's your experience? In what ways can someone's tongue direct her life? _____

_____

Although the tongue is very small, its effects on others can be large and lasting. List some of the effects your words can have on other people. _____

_____

_____

❀ Power for Good and Evil

What does the Word say? In James 3:6, with what does the writer compare the power of the tongue?

- ❏ Flood
- ❏ Fire
- ❏ Hurricane
- ❏ Blizzard

Me and My Big Mouth

What do you think? Why do you think the Bible uses this analogy?____

_____

Think about it: Have you ever seen a piece of land after a fire has swept through? If so, you know that there is nothing left standing. Every living thing is destroyed, whether plants, trees, or even human lives. The things people worked so hard to erect are burned down to a pile of ash. Fire is the most destructive force on earth. It has the power to destroy and kill.

How does the tongue have power to destroy and kill? _____

_____

What's your experience? Has there been a time when you used your words to destroy? If so, describe that instance. _____

_____

_____

Think about it: As you read the description about fire, you may have also remembered some of the positive uses of fire. With fire we warm our houses, cook our food, and light dark places. Just as fire has the potential to harm and destroy, it can also enhance our lives. You see, fire is a neutral force. When it is used with wisdom and caution, it helps people. But when it is used without discretion, it can kill. The power of the tongue is the same way. It can shape our destinies as well as the destinies of others. This is why it is so important to harness the power of the tongue.

123

List some of the ways the power of the tongue can be used for good.

_____

_____

_____

What's your experience? Describe a time when someone's words built

you up._____

_____

_____

_____

❖ Our Words Reveal Our Hearts

Fill in the blanks: Reread James 3:10 and fill in the missing words: "Out
of the same mouth come _____ and _____. My
brothers, this should not be."

What do you think? Why do you think our words sometimes honor
God and at other times dishonor Him?

Fill in the blanks: Read Jesus' words in Matthew 12:34 and fill in the
missing words: "For out of the overflow of the _____ the
_____ speaks."

Think about it: This verse shows us the true reason our words are often
less than sweet. Our words are the most accurate revelation of what
is truly inside our hearts. If you are like me, this may be scary to you.
All too often stinging and hurtful words reveal my heart.

Me and My Big Mouth

Thankfully, God never leaves us alone. As we yield to Him in obedience and are changed by the study of His Word, we will find that our hearts begin to change.

❀ **Inner Change:** Maybe as you have read this study, God has shown you areas where you need to change. Possibly you've seen how your words tear others down. We can destroy by the way we talk *to* others or even how we talk *about* them. The Bible refers to this kind of talk as gossip.

What does the Word say? Read Ephesians 4:29. According to this passage, does gossip fit the description for the way Christians should talk? Explain. _____

_____

_____

_____

What's your experience? Are there ways you use your tongue that need to change? If so, list those. _____

_____

_____

_____

_____

Friends—Study Guide

Think about it: Change takes time and cooperation with the Holy Spirit, but it is possible with God's power. It may not come overnight, but it will begin as you allow God to change you from the inside out. Others may oppose your desire to change, trying to lure you into gossip or cursing, so you may need to take drastic measures in order to reject sinful patterns. This may mean you end some conversations. Others may not understand at first but will later notice the definite change in you.

✔ **Try This:** Reread the verse we read as we began our study, Psalm 19:14. Take a few minutes to write out this verse on a card or poster board. Now post it someplace you will see it each day. This may be your bathroom mirror, your locker, or even on the ceiling above your bed. Every time you see this verse, sincerely make it your prayer to God. For you see, as God changes our hearts, our words will quickly follow.

Now add these three steps to your daily routine to help you change the way you use your tongue.

1. *Prayer*—Commit to pray daily about how you use your words.
2. *Accountability*—Ask someone to pray with you and ask you regularly about your growth in this area.
3. *Awareness of His presence*—Remind yourself that even though you cannot see God, He is constantly with you, hearing your thoughts and words.

Me and My Big Mouth

✝ Living the Word

• Reread Ephesians 4:29. List the qualifications for a Christian's speech._____

_____

_____

Now describe what would happen if you went one entire day when the only words you spoke fit this description. _____

_____

_____

_____

• Read Psalm 39:1. What do you think the Bible means by putting a "muzzle" on our mouths? _____

_____

_____

_____

How can you put a muzzle on your mouth to protect you from sinning in ways you have before? _____

_____

_____

_____

_____

Dear Point Of Grace,

I am eighteen years old, and I just started my first year in college. I am sad and lonely, and I am having a difficult time making friends. I feel like I have to wear so many masks. I think I look happy and successful on the outside, but I feel just the opposite on the inside. It's getting hard to hide my real feelings. I have hidden them so long that I am not even sure what I feel anymore. I feel I have lost who I am. How can anyone be my friend when I don't know who I am?

Rhonda

*I praise you because I am fearfully
and wonderfully made.*
Psalm 139:14 NIV

Growing the Real You

Figuring out who *you* are may be the most challenging part of being a friend to someone else. And this means taking an honest look at yourself—looking at who you are now and who you want to become. As you work through this devotional, I really want you to believe that with God's help, you can be all He intends for you to be.

First, let's think about who you are right now. What words define and describe you? Words like...daughter, sister, student, dancer, brain, Christian, blonde, pretty, athletic, friend, listener, talker, moody, laid back. This list could go on and on. Take a minute right now to write down ten words that describe you. Think about your appearance, your personality, and your spiritual life.

I, _____, am

(Write your full name here.)

Friends—Terry

1. _____
2. _____
3. _____
4. _____
5. _____
6. _____
7. _____
8. _____
9. _____
10. _____

You are the only girl like you in all of the world, so don't try to be like someone else. How boring it would be if we were all alike. Just be the best *you* that you can be. God made each one of us with unique qualities that can be used for His purposes. King David said in Psalm 139:14, "I praise you because I am fearfully and wonderfully made" (NIV). Another psalm says of God: "Your hands made me and formed me" (119:73 NIV). Do you hear the message of these verses? You are "wonderfully" made, and *God* is the one who made you—on purpose! Learn to celebrate your uniqueness.

I am so glad that the four of us in Point Of Grace all have different personalities. I think that is what has kept us sane over the eleven years we've been singing together. Shelley has a leader, take-charge kind of personality. Heather is laid back and passionate. Denise is energetic and outgoing, and I am organized and empathetic.

Growing the Real You

Our group has worked well *because* we are all so different. It is our four unique sets of talents and personalities that make Point Of Grace the group that it is. Our theme verses could be 1 Corinthians 12:4–6 which say, "There are different kinds of gifts, but the same Spirit. There are different kinds of service, but the same Lord. There are different kinds of working, but the same God works all of them in all men" (NIV).

You are the only one just like you. Learn to relax in the good things you are. Stop comparing yourself to others. Be comfortable with your looks, your quirks, and your surroundings. You are unique. Enjoy it! Be yourself and allow others to be themselves.

Now that we've talked a little about who you are as an individual, let's tackle the difficult part of this discussion. Let's take a minute to talk about *change*. In order to be the best friend you can be—and the best person—you'll probably need to make some changes. And the kind of changes I want us to focus on are *character* changes. Character is who you are on the inside—the part of you that's still there when no one else is looking. Character qualities include things like honesty, loyalty, kindness, joy, and patience. And the good thing about character traits is that all of us can grow and develop these traits in ourselves, no matter what our personalities are like.

In a way, thinking about change is not so difficult—especially at this stage of your life. The years between ages thirteen and twenty are *full* of change. You are experiencing new emotions; you are figuring out who you are and what life is about. This time of life is filled with exciting possibilities. You can actually make a plan for who you want to become and set out to become it.

Are you the person today that you want to be ten years from now? Think about the qualities that make up a good friend—not only a good friend but also a good person—and write them below. If you'll start working on the person you want to become *now*, you can drastically affect who you will be. Here's some ideas to help you get started. A good friend is honest, forgiving, godly, encouraging, loyal, a good listener, available, giving, genuine, and fun. Also think of what a friend is not: gossipy, critical, cliquish, or out to impress others. Now list the character traits you want to have in your life. (And try not to just copy the things I listed. Think about who *you* want to be.)

I, _____, want to be:

(Write your full name here.)

1. _____

2. _____

3. _____

4. _____

5. _____

6. _____

7. _____

8. _____

9. _____

10. _____

Growing the Real You

Remember and hold on to this statement made by the apostle Paul: "I can do all things through Christ who strengthens me" (Philippians 4:13 NKJV). Choose one or two traits to work on each week, and set your mind to changing for the better. God will give you the strength to do it.

You'll be more purposeful and effective in your efforts to change if you'll write about your progress in a journal. (You could use the *Girls Of Grace* journal!) Write about your daily commitment to become the person God wants you to be, and write about your struggles along the way. Remind yourself in every circumstance that you want to be a godly girl and focus on doing what is right. You can do it! Have confidence that if you have done a little thing well, you can do a bigger thing well, too.

Billy Graham, who is one of my heroes, in talking about identity crises in youth, said that the "chief symptom is the cry: 'Who am I?' To them I say, 'Have a confrontation with yourself. Then have a confrontation with Jesus Christ.'" I love that.

My dad used to tell me and my three sisters that we were beautiful on the inside, and honestly, that felt better than when he said I was beautiful on the outside. Becoming beautiful on the inside takes hard work, and when someone notices how much work you put into being a godly girl, that means the world.

Have you ever seen a woman or girl who is beautiful on the outside…until she opens her mouth and says something ugly? At that moment, her beauty vanishes. I have seen bitterness and jealousy eat away at outwardly beautiful people until they were actually ugly.

Friends—Terry

Last year I saw the movie *Shallow Hal*, and I wish I could see people the way Hal did. Hal's perspective about people totally changed from the beginning of the movie to the end. He had a powerful encounter with a famous speaker and dramatically was changed. Before this encounter, he judged every girl by her outward appearance; but afterward, he saw only the inner person—the heart. Some women, who were beautiful on the outside, all of a sudden were ugly and gross. He ends up falling in love with a really overweight girl because with his new perspective, he saw only her beautiful, "supermodel" heart. The poet Robert Frost said, "The only lasting beauty is the beauty of the heart." There's a lot of truth in that statement.

Lisa Ryans, in her book *For Such a Time As This*, uses the word *friendship* in place of *love* in 1 Corinthians 13:4–8 so that it reads:

Friendship is very patient and kind, never jealous or envious, never boastful or proud, never haughty or selfish or rude. Friendship does not demand its own way. It is not irritable or touchy. It does not hold a grudge and will hardly even notice when others do it wrong. If you love someone [as a friend], you will be loyal to her no matter what the cost. You will always believe in her, always expect the best of her, and always stand your ground in defending her. The love of a Godly friend…endures through every circumstance.

Remember, the inner beauty of your heart and soul will shine farther than any outer beauty ever could. Start today to become the kind of person and friend God wants you to be.

Growing the Real You

One of the girls I meet with at my church found this poem engraved on a park bench in Texas.

Some people come into our lives and quickly go.
Some people move our souls to dance;
They awaken us to a new understanding with the passing of their wisdom.
Some people make the sky more beautiful to gaze upon;
They stay in our lives for a while, leave footprints on our hearts,
And we are never, ever the same.

I want to be that to someone, don't you?

STUDY GUIDE

Am I a True Friend?

📖 **Opening Scripture:** Please begin by reading 1 Peter 3:15. Ask God to speak to you today as you study His Word.

❀ **What Is a True Friend?** What thoughts come to your mind when you hear the word *friend?* You may immediately picture someone you know who has been a faithful and caring friend. Maybe you think of characteristics demonstrated by a true friend.

What does it mean? In your own words, define the word *friend.* _____

_____

_____

_____

What do you think? In your opinion, what is the most important thing someone can do for her friend?

❑ Keep her secrets.

❑ Make memories together.

❑ Share Christ with her.

❑ Loan her money.

❀ **God's Ambassadors:** Second Corinthians 5:20 says, "We are therefore Christ's ambassadors, as though God were making his appeal through us."

Am I a True Friend?

What does it mean? The dictionary definition of an *ambassador* is "a special representative or an official agent with a special mission."

What do you think? If you are a Christian, you are sent into the world with a special mission. In what ways do you think God wants to use you to fulfill His mission in the lives of your friends? _____

_____

_____

_____

✿ **Sharing What's Truly Valuable:** Look back at your definition for the word *friend*.

What's your experience? Write about a past experience when someone offered you true friendship._____

_____

_____

If you've ever had a friend who was in need of food or money, what did you do? _____

_____

Why do you think it is so easy to share our *things* with others but so hard to share our personal relationship with Jesus?_____

_____

_____

Friends—Study Guide

Have you ever made an effort to share about Jesus Christ with friends? If so, how did it go? _____

_____

_____

Pray about it: If you have friends who don't personally know Jesus Christ, you can be sure God has placed them in your life so you can be a witness. Can you think of two friends who do not know Christ? If so, write their names in the following space and commit to pray-ing for them daily: _____

_____

_____

❧ **What's Holding You Back?** If you have friends who don't know Jesus but haven't talked to them about your faith, what is holding you back?

    ❏ I am waiting to understand more about the Bible before I share with them.

    ❏ I am scared of what they will think about me.

    ❏ I am waiting for the best time to share with them.

    ❏ I know that they will reject Jesus and His love.

There are many things that hold us back from sharing His love.

1. Knowledge: Some people think they need to understand the com-plete truth of the Bible before they witness to others. If this were correct, no one would ever share. Not even the most eloquent preacher can fully understand the mysteries of God's Word.

God doesn't call us to know everything before we open our mouths; instead, He calls us to share what we do know with those He has placed in our lives. God used the uneducated disciples to spread His truth. He wants to use you. Are you willing? Why or why not?

_____

_____

_____

_____

2. Fear: The second excuse people use is that they are scared of what others will think about them. Have you ever used this excuse? If so, how can you overcome your fear of what others think? _____

_____

_____

_____

_____

3. Timing: Sometimes people say that they are waiting until an ideal time before they witness to someone. While this may be true, it is often just a way of putting off obedience to God. Have you ever been guilty of putting off sharing your faith with another person? If so, how can you overcome the tendency to put off obedience? _____

_____

_____

_____

4. Rejection: The last excuse people use is to claim they know the person will reject Christ. The problem with this excuse is that we cannot read another's mind. You may share with someone who looks like she has no need for Jesus but on the inside is dying to hear about Christ's love.

❀ **Preparing to Share:** Reread 1 Peter 3:15. What does this verse teach that we must do before we share?

❏ Become knowledgeable about the Bible

❏ Put Christ first in our lives

❏ Pray for three or four hours that God will use our words

❏ Understand everything our friends believe

What do you think? Why is it important that Christ is first place in our lives if we are to be effective witnesses for Him? _____

_____

_____

_____

The passage teaches that we should always be ready to share about Christ. How can you be ready at all times to share with another about your relationship with Jesus? _____

_____

Am I a True Friend?

_____

_____

❖ **A Distinct Life:** A Christian's life should be distinct enough that it stands out to unbelievers. They should wonder what is different about us. Christians should have an unusual hope that is not found in the world.

What's your experience? Does your life demonstrate to unbelievers that you have hope? If so, how?_____

_____

_____

_____

What does the Word say? Read Matthew 5:14–16. Jesus compares Christians to a:

- ❏ Lighthouse
- ❏ Boat
- ❏ Bird
- ❏ Light

Think about it: We shouldn't try to draw attention to ourselves so that people will praise us for our goodness; rather, we should point them to Jesus. Our goal should be that others turn their lives over to Christ and praise our Father in heaven. Just as light in a dark room helps us find our way, we are to be the light that helps others find the way to Christ.

In what ways can you let your light shine before men? _____

_____

_____

_____

❧ **Become a True Friend:** Will you commit to become a true friend? Will you be the kind of friend who not only shares memories and secrets, but who also shares how to find eternal life through Jesus Christ? If you discovered the cure for a disease and your friend contracted that very disease, you would most certainly share the cure. As a Christian, you have the good news of forgiveness and life in Jesus Christ. Whatever you do, don't keep it to yourself!

✔ **Try This:** Make a list of those in your circle of friends. Next to each person's name, write something you can pray about for that person this week. Next, put a star by those who need to hear about Jesus' love. Pray over your list this week, asking God to open doors for you to share with those who do not know about Him. When the opportunities arise, take them. Don't be ashamed about what Jesus has done in your life. _____

_____

_____

Am I a True Friend?

_____

✝ **Living the Word:** Read Colossians 4:5–6.

• In what ways can you be wise in the way you act toward outsiders?

_____

_____

• List some of the situations you will be in this week where unbelievers will be present. _____

_____

• What would happen if you made the most of every opportunity
God gives you to share about Him this week?_____

_____

• Describe what conversation "full of grace" and "seasoned with
salt" is like. _____

_____

_____

• What practical steps can you take so that your conversation fits
this description? _____

_____

_____

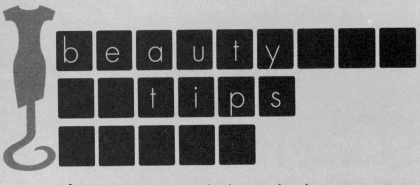

beauty tips

❀ Use cold water for a final rinse after shampooing to make hair extra shiny.

❀ Keep your hands off your face. Most zits develop by the transference of oil, dirt, and germs on your hands to your face.

❀ Never go on a "crash" diet. If you feel the need to lose weight, begin a well-balanced diet: Cut out sweets and junk food and add lots of fruits and vegetables. Choose steamed or roasted over fried. Leave off the gravy. Reduce the portions of what you eat for your three main meals and add healthy snacks in-between to boost your metabolism and keep you from getting hungry.

❀ Exercise. It's great not only for the body but also for the mind. It releases stress, helps you think more clearly, gives you energy, and helps you feel better about yourself.

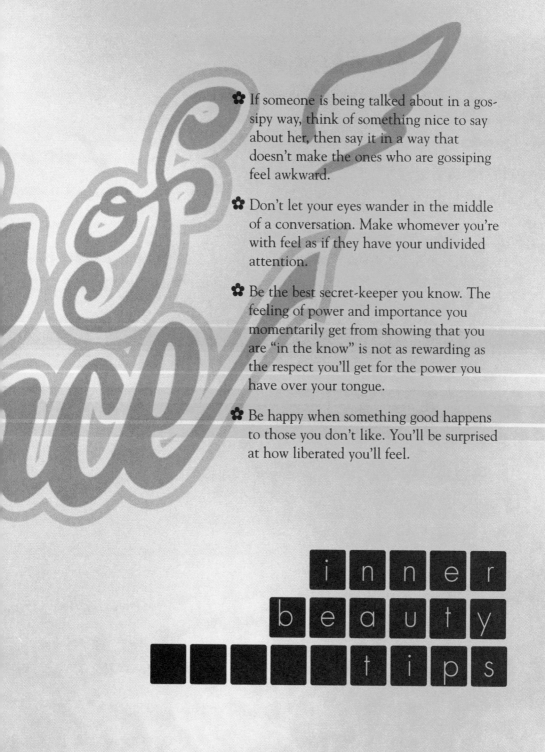

✿ If someone is being talked about in a gossipy way, think of something nice to say about her, then say it in a way that doesn't make the ones who are gossiping feel awkward.

✿ Don't let your eyes wander in the middle of a conversation. Make whomever you're with feel as if they have your undivided attention.

✿ Be the best secret-keeper you know. The feeling of power and importance you momentarily get from showing that you are "in the know" is not as rewarding as the respect you'll get for the power you have over your tongue.

✿ Be happy when something good happens to those you don't like. You'll be surprised at how liberated you'll feel.

inner beauty tips

Denise

b♥ys

Dear Point Of Grace,

I am going out with the most wonderful guy. He's so perfect for me! We like the same things like movies and music and sports, and we even have the same favorite foods and colors! But more than all that, I love the way he makes me feel that I am special—he says that nobody has ever made him feel the way I make him feel.

The more I'm with him, the more I want to be with him. The only problem is that I'm afraid I've let the physical part of our relationship get out of control, and I don't know how to stop it. It's easy to be strong when I'm away from him, but as soon as we're together, I lose control. I'm a Christian, and I feel bad for doing things I shouldn't. But how can I stop now that I've gone this far? Some of my friends say that if a girl does what I've done, she isn't a virgin anymore. Should I even try to stop if my friends are right that it's too late for me, anyway?

Mary

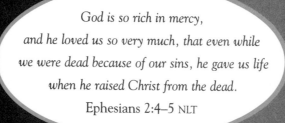

*God is so rich in mercy,
and he loved us so very much, that even while
we were dead because of our sins, he gave us life
when he raised Christ from the dead.*

Ephesians 2:4–5 NLT

Our Desire for Love

The desire to be accepted and part of a group is deep within the hearts of all of us. We want to be noticed. We want to be *loved*.

But in our search for love and acceptance, we tend to look everywhere but up. God's love for us is unconditional and unending, yet we hunger for acceptance and affirmation from the people around us—especially the male version of people.

I have always liked boys. When I was two, I wanted to be a boy. When I was in kindergarten, I kissed my first boy underneath a table. But it was in junior high that I first started looking to guys for the special attention that up to then I'd found in my girlfriends, my family, and God. Until then, guys were really just good friends. I loved sports, so I loved hanging out with guys. We were buddies, and I liked it that way. But then I started noticing that all my girlfriends had boyfriends, and I began to wonder what was wrong with me. Why didn't I have a boyfriend?

In the movies, the female lead always had the cutest boyfriend. The magazines I read highlighted who was dating whom and how to find Mr. Right. My girlfriends began trying to help me find someone to "go with." The pressure to have a special someone seemed to come from everywhere. We live in a world that teaches us that "love" can be found by being the cutest, smartest, sexiest, or skinniest.

It's only natural to want the attention of the opposite sex. What girl doesn't want someone special to call her every night? Who doesn't like having someone to be giggly about at a slumber party? It's fun! When I was your age, it was much easier to get up in the morning and get ready for school when I knew I would see that cute guy in second period. Have you been there?

The problem is that in my search for attention from guys, I became distracted from my devotion to God. I lost sight of the big picture of who I was and what God wanted for me. I began to play the games that many of you play: You think a boy is cute, so you tell your best friend to tell his best friend and then somehow you end up "going out." "Going where?" my parents used to say. It would make me so mad!

After "going with" a few guys for maybe two weeks at a time, I finally got my first real boyfriend. It was the end of summer break, and I was registering for the tenth grade. This guy and I had been friends in the ninth grade, but I'll never forget seeing him in the registration line. The sparks flew! He even had his own truck, and he looked so cute driving it!

Our Desire for Love

He seemed perfect! He was a Christian, he loved God, and he was very involved with FCA (that's Fellowship of Christian Athletes). I wanted to spend every waking moment with him. We saw each other at school, church, football games, basketball games, FCA meetings—it was awesome!

But soon, the fire and passion I'd had for God in the seventh, eighth, and ninth grades became more of a flicker, and my passion for my boyfriend grew into a flame. Neither of us meant to do anything wrong. We didn't deliberately set out to disobey God. But it wasn't long before our physical relationship became less than innocent. We never "went all the way," but we did cross some lines I wish we hadn't.

I wish, now, that I had talked to someone I trusted right from the very start of our relationship—my youth minister's wife, my Sunday school teacher, even my parents. But I was too embarrassed and proud to tell them of my struggles. If I'd been honest, I know that any one of them would have helped me and saved me some regret.

Satan has a tricky way of turning down our "sin-sensitivity" level. You know what I mean. The first time you step over a line, you feel that twinge of guilt in your stomach telling you that what you're doing isn't right. But the next time you do it, you're not quite so sensitive to the conviction. It gets easier and easier to ignore, and pretty soon you don't feel it at all.

The Bible says that sexual sin is different from any other kind of sin: "Run away from sexual sin! No other sin so clearly affects the body as this one does. For sexual immorality is a sin against your own body" (1 Corinthians 6:18 NLT). It's different because when we share that kind of intimacy with another person, we become "one" with that person; but God wants us to be one spirit with *Him* (see 1 Corinthians 6:16–17).

God has wired us to need intimacy and love (we'll talk more about that in the next devotional), but Satan perverts that need so that we look for it in all the wrong places—and sexual intimacy outside of marriage is one of the places too many girls look.

Maybe you are one of those girls. Or maybe you've never been asked to contemplate how you act on a date. Some kids think that if they abstain from the "technical" act of sex, doing everything else is OK. This way of thinking may keep you from getting pregnant, but it isn't "OK" with God, and the spiritual and psychological damage can be just as severe as "going all the way." Studies show that Christian kids struggle with these issues just as much as non-Christians do.

But it's important to know that it's never too late to make things right—no matter what you've done in the past.

There really is no such thing as a "good girl." The Bible says that "all have sinned; all fall short of God's glorious standard" (Romans 3:23 NLT). No one—not even the most godly girl you know—can stand before God on her own merit. It is only by the grace of God, extended to us through the blood of Jesus, that we are made pure.

Did you know that the word *virgin* means "pure"? You can be pure, even now. With God's help, you can be pure in the way you think and the way you act, the way you dress and the way you carry yourself. Your relationship with guys in the future can be all new. You can be a virgin in every sense but the "technical" one.

Whether you've been looking for love in sexual relationships or in acceptance from friends or excellence in school or sports, you can turn your heart back to God and find the love you yearn for in Him.

When we trust Jesus as our sacrificial Lamb, His precious blood washes all our sins away. First John 1:7 says that when we walk in the light of Jesus, His blood cleanses us from all sin. Sin makes us feel dirty. Jesus can make us clean. Wouldn't you like to feel clean all over? A great book called *Intimate Issues* by Linda Dillow and Lorraine Pintus shares the following ideas:

Step into the shower of confession. Your "heart cleansing" starts by being open and honest with God. Tell Him every detail. Tell Him what your heart is chasing after. Confess to Him any sexual sin ("If we confess our sins, he is faithful and just and will forgive us our sins and purify us from *all unrighteousness*" 1 John 1:9 NIV). You can do this by yourself, or you can ask a special friend (not your boyfriend!) to pray with you as you confess to the Lord.

Soak in a bubble bath of His love. Sometimes this is as hard as the confession process because we don't feel we deserve God's love. We have a hard time believing that He could love us in spite of our sin. But He does. Immerse yourself in His love and accept His forgiveness. He also wants you to forgive yourself. Look at these Scriptures and soak in their promises. If you struggle a lot with feeling guilty, these would be good for you to memorize: "'Their sins and lawless acts I will remember no more.' And where these have been forgiven, there is no longer any sacrifice for sin" (Hebrews 10:17–18 NIV). "'Then neither do I condemn you' Jesus declared. 'Go now and leave your life of sin'" (John 8:11 NIV). "For I will forgive their wickedness and will remember their sins no more" (Hebrews 8:12 NIV). "Everyone who has this hope in him purifies himself, just as he is pure" (1 John 3:3 NIV). "Forget the former things; do not dwell on the past. See, I am doing a new thing! Now it springs up; do you not perceive it? I am making a way in the desert and streams in the wasteland. I, even I, am he who blots out your transgressions, for my own sake, and remembers our sins no more" (Isaiah 43:18–19, 25 NIV).

Put on some new clothes. Isaiah 61:10 says, "I am overwhelmed with joy in the LORD my God! For he has dressed me with the clothing of salvation and draped me in a robe of righteousness" (NLT). All I can say to that is "Wow!" (You might even want to buy yourself something special to celebrate your renewal—I always welcome a reason to shop.) Philippians 3:12–14 gives us hope for new beginnings: "Not that I have already obtained all this, or have already been made perfect, but I press on to take hold of that for which Christ Jesus took hold of me. Brothers, (or sisters) I do not consider myself yet to have taken hold of it. but one thing I do: Forgetting what is behind and straining toward what is ahead, I press on toward the goal to win the prize for which God has called me heavenward in Christ Jesus" (NIV).

And we can celebrate with this verse in Romans 4:7–8: "Blessed are they whose transgressions are forgiven, whose sins are covered. Blessed is the man whose sin the Lord will never count against him" (NIV).

Our Desire for Love

Now let's think back to the reason we are drawn to boys in the first place. It's because we desire to be loved. Well, we are! God loved you so much that He sent His Son to die for your sins. He did this so that you can someday be in heaven with Him and live with Him forever! If God loves you this much, don't you think He will provide for your every need? Stop trying to be God in your life. It takes a lot of pressure off.

Maybe sex is not a struggle for you. Maybe you struggle with friends, grades, clothes, or your appearance. What controls you? In a book called *Out of the Saltshaker*, Rebecca Peppert writes, "Whatever controls us is our lord. The person who seeks power is controlled by power. The person who seeks acceptance is controlled by acceptance. We do not control ourselves. We are controlled by the lord of our lives."

Make sure that you are looking for love in the right place. Make sure that Jesus is the Lord of your life. I encourage you to sit down and think about what is most important to you. Talk to God about it. Ask Him to help you make Him first in your life. For me, it's not something I can do once. It's a daily effort of seeking Him. The good news is that He is always pursuing you—and He will never stop.

becoming a girl of grace

becoming a girl of grace

STUDY GUIDE

My First Love

Opening Scripture: Begin by reading Matthew 22:36–38. This may be a familiar passage to you, so ask God to give you a heart to hear from Him in a new way today.

❧ **First Love:** We have all dreamed about someday falling in love. We read about it in books and see it in movies. We anticipate the day we'll meet someone special and our lives will never be the same.

Think about it: What do you look forward to the most about falling in love someday? _____

_____

_____

Did you know that God wants to be the very first love of your life, before any other person? How does that make you feel?_____

_____

Does it make you feel incredibly valued and special? It should. The God of the entire universe desires for you to love Him first. What an amazing thought.

❧ **He Wants *All* of You:** How can we make God our first love? Let's look at Matthew 22:37 again to find out.

Fill in the blanks: "Jesus replied: 'Love the Lord your God with _____ your heart and with _____ your soul and with _____ your mind.'"

My First Love

Think about it: The key word here is *all*. God isn't content for us to bring Him the leftover parts of ourselves after we've given our love elsewhere. He wants to be our first love.

The first part of the verse talks about loving the Lord with all your heart. This means we must guard against giving first place to anyone other than God. Only He should occupy first place.

Take some time to think about your own heart. What person or thing has first place right now?

❏ My family and friends

❏ Finding happiness for myself

❏ God

❏ Other: _____.

✿ All of Your Heart

Think about it: If God isn't the first love in your heart right now, what are some practical steps you can take to change that? _____

_____

_____

_____

What does the Word say? Read Psalm 73:25–26.

Have you ever stumbled upon a love letter or e-mail that was very personal and private? In a sense, Psalm 73 is a love letter in which Asaph, the writer, pours his heart out to God.

Boys—Study Guide

What is the writer saying to God in this psalm?

❏ "God, I know You aren't in first place now, but someday You will be."

❏ "God, please help me to get out of the mess I am in."

❏ "God, You fill my heart in a way that no one else can."

❏ "God, help me to understand You more."

Fill in the blanks: Read Psalm 73:26 and fill in the missing words. "My flesh and my heart may fail, but God is the _____ of my heart and my _____ forever."

What do you think? What do you think the writer means by "My flesh and my heart may fail"? _____

_____

What is meant by the phrase "strength of my heart"? _____

_____

What's your experience? Has there ever been a time when you found the strength of your heart in God? If so, describe that experience._____

_____

_____

Think about it: Every word matters in a love letter. The writer chooses words that hold special meaning. In using the word *portion*, Asaph simply means that God satisfies Him. In a sense it is like when you are satisfied by a hearty meal; you are completely full, not wanting for more.

My First Love

Can you honestly make the same declaration as the psalmist, that your relationship with God satisfies you in a way no other relationship does? Explain your answer. _____

_____

_____

_____

_____

_____

✿ All of Your Soul

Think about it: In Matthew 22:37, Jesus also calls us to love God with all of our souls. Your soul is the part of you made up of will and emotions. It determines your behavior. Knowing this, why is it so important that we love God with our souls? _____

_____

_____

_____

_____

Fill in the blanks: Read Colossians 1:16 and fill in the missing words. "For by him all things were created: things in heaven and on earth, visible and invisible, whether thrones or powers or rulers or authorities; _____ _____ were created _____ him and _____ him."

What does the Word say? Now look closely at the last part of the verse. Why were all things created?

❑ Because God needed to spend some time on something, so why not creating?

❑ For Him

❑ For there to be something to study in history class

❑ For the beauty of the earth

According to this verse, what was God's purpose in creating you?

_____

_____

_____

What's your experience? In what ways can you choose to live *for Him?*

_____

_____

_____

❀ All of Your Mind

Think about it: In Matthew 22:37, Jesus calls us to love Him with all of our minds. We often think of love in terms of our heart or choices, while we rarely think of it as an act of our minds.

What does the Word say? Let's read Exodus 20:4–5 and see what we can learn. This passage comes straight from the Ten Commandments. God tells His people He is jealous for them. He commands them to worship no other person or thing. God doesn't want thoughts about others to occupy greater space in our minds than our thoughts about Him.

What's your experience? In what ways have you been guilty of placing others ahead of God in your mind? _____

_____

Think about it: One way we do this is by allowing our thoughts to be captivated by another person or thing. We must guard what we allow into our minds because wrong thoughts can eventually become strongholds over us.

In what ways can you guard the things you allow into your mind?

_____

_____

❧ **Only God Can Meet Your Deepest Needs:** God created us with needs for love, acceptance, and security, but we must allow Him to meet those primary needs before going to anyone else. No human love can fill up those empty places inside of you. You must never allow yourself to believe someone else can meet needs only God can meet.

What's your experience? Has there ever been a time when you looked to someone else to meet needs that only God could meet? If so, what happened? _____

_____

_____

_____

✔ **Try This:** Take a few moments to examine the loves of your heart today. Will you commit to love God with all your heart, soul, and mind? If so, every other love will be put in its proper place. Are there some changes you need to make? If so, what action steps are you going to take to make those a reality?_____

_____

_____

_____

_____

_____

_____

✝ **Living the Word:** Reread Psalm 73:25–26.

• The writer has a strong appetite for intimacy with God. He says his desire for God surpasses all other desires. What about you? Do your appetites for other things surpass your appetite for God? If so, what changes will you make? _____

_____

_____

_____

_____

My First Love

_____

_____

• Other people may love you fully, but only God can love you perfectly. God is the only One who will never fail you. Write a prayer of thanksgiving to Him. You may want to get ideas from Psalm 73 for your love letter to Him. _____

_____

_____

_____

_____

_____

_____

_____

Dear Point Of Grace,

I heard something the other day about how Christians my age shouldn't date until they're ready to get married—that they should "court" instead. I really want to do what's right, but I've been going out with boys ever since sixth grade, and dating doesn't seem like such a serious deal as they're trying to make it out to be. I don't have a boyfriend at the moment, and I feel kinda left out without one. Plus, I'm afraid that I won't have a date to the prom (which is what I really want!).

Sometimes I think I might be happy just hanging with my guy friends, but some of them want to be "friends with benefits" (you know, where you just kiss for fun), so I might as well have a boyfriend. What do you think?

Stephanie

So whether you eat or drink or
whatever you do,
do it all for the glory of God.
1 Corinthians 10:31 NIV

The Dating Dilemma

Dating has become quite *the* discussion in Christian circles. Should people date? Or should they court? What about holding hands or kissing? What's right? What's wrong? What difference does it all make?

When I first heard about the book by Joshua Harris called *I Kissed Dating Goodbye*, my first reaction was, "This is a little extreme, don't ya think?" However, after reading it and the author's next book, *Boy Meets Girl*, I have some different thoughts on the subject.

I realized that what really matters is not whether we date or court—what really matters is, *Are we listening to God? Are we glorifying Him in our relationships?* This main issue is not even boy-girl relationships—it's more about how we love and respect others—all others—not just boys. The real question is, *Do I encourage those I know to love and trust God more?*

165

Boys—Denise

As I think back over the guys I dated in high school and college, I realize that that question didn't even enter my mind. I never asked, "Lord, how can a relationship with this guy draw me closer to You, and how can I show him how great You are?" Josh Harris says that if we *really* care for someone, we would think about what's best for his relationship with Christ. If we would put on the mind of Christ in any relationship, imagine how much more we would care for others!

Now, I'm not encouraging "missionary dating" (that's dating someone who is not a Christian in hopes of bringing them to Christ). In fact, I highly advise against dating a non-Christian. Sure, every now and then a non-Christian guy will come to know the Lord while dating a Christian girl, but the odds are *very* low.

You need to know that it is not your responsibility to make your boyfriend walk obediently with God. I often thought that I was the moral police for the guys I dated. But in reality, the guys you date are responsible for making their own choices. If you don't agree with those choices, then maybe you should rethink the relationship. You don't have to be judgmental, but some of their wrong choices can affect you and drag you down. In those cases, it might be better just to be friends.

High school can be such a fun part of life, so why does dating have to complicate everything so much? It goes back to the issue of what we are searching for and who we find our security in. The problem is that being intimate (like kissing, hugging, holding hands, and a lot more) has become so common with people your age that it seems odd when that's not part of a relationship.

The Dating Dilemma

Is there something wrong with just being great friends? Can't you still go out to movies, football games, and concerts? We often think we have to do more.

Whether you decide to date or not, it's important to listen to God's voice. As I sat with a group of girls in my living room recently, I asked them what they thought about dating and courting. Most of them still wanted to date. So, if that is the case with you, there are several good guidelines to help you through the dating process. One excellent book is *I Gave Dating a Chance* by Jeramy Clark. I'd also like to share the following ideas:

Pray about it. What's the first thing you should do if there's a particular guy you want to get to know better? When I was a teen, the first thing I did was try to be around the guy and flirt to make him notice me. But I was wrong. The first thing I should have done was pray about it and tell God how I felt.

Examine your motives. The next thing I should have done was ask myself why I wanted to be with the guy so much. Did I want to date him just to make myself look good? Was I feeling left out and just wanted *someone* to date so I'd fit in with everyone else? Even if he's a really neat Christian guy and you have a lot in common, make sure that your motives are right. And remember, you don't have to date a guy to have him as a friend. Many of the best guy-girl relationships are *friendships*.

Trust God with your future. Why do we find it so hard to trust God with our future? I remember having my life all mapped out in high school—the marriage, the kids, the kind of jobs we would have. I was in the eleventh grade! I had no idea what path God would take me on during the next ten years. Why did I feel like it was so important to know all this stuff? Think about it—how often do we try to *make* things happen? We try to be matchmakers instead of letting the Maker make the match. (Girls are the worst about this!) I remember walking by the gym about the time I knew practice was over just so I could run into a certain guy "by chance." We were always trying to push our guy friends into telling us whom they asked to the prom. We are *so nosy!* We are the ones forcing guys to ask girls out. If we left them alone, many relationships would probably never start, and fewer people would end up getting hurt by breakups.

Be accountable to others. OK. Let's say you've checked your motives and you think you're on track. Now let's say that he asks you out. What do you do next? Well, after you climb off the ceiling and call your girlfriends, you really need to stop and pray about it again. Talk to people other than just your girlfriends— like your parents, Sunday school teacher, or youth minister. See what they think, and if it all seems right, then say "yes," but make sure you proceed with caution. Set boundaries and plan ahead. You can't wait until you're with a guy in a parked car somewhere to decide that's not a good thing.

Get your parents involved in some of these decisions. If they don't set a curfew, make a reasonable one for yourself. Talk to them and share your heart about having a godly relationship. There is no one on earth I would rather not disappoint than my parents. If you are blessed with godly parents, welcome it. But even if they're not Christian parents, most of them want you to have boundaries and dating guidelines because they love you.

It's good to have an accountability relationship with your godly girlfriends. I know a precious girl who is part of an accountability group. They pray for each other before dates and call each other with the details after the date. (If you do this, make sure your conversation doesn't become a gossip session.) If you're in junior high or high school, I also suggest you share the details of your date with an adult. When you know you're going to give an honest report to someone, you are less likely to stray from your principles. I wish I'd had someone to share my struggles with—it would have changed a lot of things for me.

Know the limits. A question that is asked a lot is, *How far is too far?* When you ask this question, make sure you're not just wanting to know how much you can get away with. I can't refer you to a verse in the Bible that says holding hands or kissing is wrong, but I do know this—God puts a conscience in each one of us, and His Holy Spirit "speaks" to us. Even kissing can be too intimate in some relationships. I also know that when we go too far, our sinful nature tends to tune out the Holy Spirit's warnings. That is why it is so important to set guidelines before you ever get into a relationship.

Don't "waste" your time on useless dates. Now, I don't mean this in a snobbish way—I mean it in a wise, prayerful way. As I look back at my dating years—especially in college—I see so many useless dates. They didn't benefit me or the guy I went out with. I was just dating to date. Many of these guys might have been fine friends, but dating them just complicated things. Make sure the relationship is "worth" the time and effort.

Be careful about praying together. Here's a heads-up: Praying alone with a guy you're dating is usually not a good idea—unless maybe it's a quick simple prayer to set the tone at the beginning of a date. Prayer is one of the most intimate of communications and can bring out all sorts of emotions.

Sometimes being spiritually intimate can lead to physical intimacy. You absolutely should pray *for* each other, but aside from a brief "before-the-date" prayer, you should do it separately or in the presence of a man or woman you respect.

Avoid influences that "stir you up" sexually. Be careful about the movies and TV shows you watch, about the music you listen to, the books you read, and the people you hang around with. All of these things can influence your thinking and tempt you to respond sinfully.

The New Living Translation of Romans 6:12–13 says this: "Do not let sin control the way you live; do not give in to its lustful desires. Do not let any part of your body become a tool of wickedness, to be used for sinning. Instead, give yourselves completely to God since you have been given new life. And use your whole body as a tool to do what is right for the glory of God."

Because we are saved, we are no longer slaves to sin. By God's grace through what Jesus did for us on the cross, we no longer have sin *ruling* over us. But unfortunately, that does not mean that sin no longer has an *influence* in our lives. That is why it's necessary to know God by reading His Word every day and surrounding ourselves with godly people. Don't place yourself in situations that you know have a strong chance for a bad outcome.

In thinking about all we've discussed, remember to always ask yourself, "Am I glorifying God in this relationship?" "Am I as concerned about my friend or boyfriend as I am about myself?" The reason we are here on earth is to glorify and fellowship with God and shine His light into the lives of those

The Dating Dilemma

around us. Remember, dating isn't just about dating—it's about looking at how we can include God in the things we do and the people we interact with.

I challenge you to take some time to evaluate the special relationships in your life. Ask God to show you how you have or haven't shown His glory through your relationships. Even though I was imperfect in many of my dating relationships, and even though I still fail my friends, my husband, and my children from time to time today; I'm thankful that God loves me perfectly and that one day we, too, will love perfectly.

Safety in Standards

📖 **Opening Scripture:** Start by praying that God would give you ears to hear and obey Him today as you study His Word. Now read Psalm 119:9.

Fill in the blanks: "How can a young man keep his way _____? By living according to your _____."

❀ **God's Word—Your Guide to Purity:** Psalm 119:9 could also apply to a "young woman." You may have asked yourself the same question that the verse asks: "How can I stay pure in this world?" It seems that walking in purity gets harder each year. Temptation seems to come from everywhere. Isn't it amazing how God's Word applies to our lives today? The questions asked thousands of years ago are still around. So are the answers; they are found in God's Word.

What does the Word say? The answer to the question is in the second part of the verse. What is it?

❑ If we try hard, we can remain pure.

❑ The only way to stay pure is to lock yourself in your room.

❑ We can stay pure if we stay in God's Word.

❑ Purity is impossible, so we should just stop trying.

Think about it: Those who walk in purity live according to the teachings and principles of God's Word. They take the Word of God seriously by learning and applying it to their lives.

Safety in Standards

What part does the Bible play in determining your behavior?

❑ The Bible has little to do with my daily life.

❑ I am growing more each day in applying God's Word to my life.

❑ I have little interest in learning more about the Bible.

❑ God's Word hasn't been a big part of my life in the past, but I want to change that.

What do you think? Why is the Bible critical if we want to live in purity?

_____

_____

_____

Think about it: The Bible is God's handbook for life. He made you for Himself and has graciously provided you His owner's manual, the Bible, to teach you how to live. In that manual, He includes instructions for every area of life. There are teachings regarding family, money, life purpose, and even love. Those who are wise read and obey His Word. They save themselves from unnecessary consequences and heartache.

❖ **The Blessings of Boundaries:** God's Word provides us boundaries for living. Although boundaries may seem inconvenient, they really save lives. If it weren't for boundaries, people would walk off of ledges or drive off dangerous roads. Have you ever been to the Grand Canyon? Everywhere you look there are railings that serve as boundaries to hold people back from the dangerous edge. They are there for safety.

What's your experience? Can you think of a boundary that has kept you safe? It may be a rule your parents have set or a principle from the Bible. List it here. _____

_____

Think about it: Setting boundaries in your dating life will protect you. Boundaries are simply decisions you make before you find yourself in a particular situation. _____

_____

What's your experience? Have you ever determined boundaries for your dating life? If so, what are they? If not, why not? _____

_____

❧ The Bible's Guidelines for Dating

1. Date Christian boys.

Fill in the blanks: Read 2 Corinthians 6:14 and fill in the missing words: "Do not be _____ together with _____. For what do _____ and wickedness have in _____? Or what fellowship can light have with _____?"

Think about it: A "yoke" joins together two oxen for the purpose of doing a particular job, such as plowing a field. The writer is using this word picture to teach that Christians must only be joined to other Christians. If you are a Christian, the only guys you should ever consider dating are other growing Christians who can challenge you in your relationship with Christ.

What do you think? What is your response to this statement?

- ❑ I want to obey God in every part of life, so I will follow this principle.
- ❑ That is crazy! Who would I date?
- ❑ I have not done this in the past, but I am willing to change.
- ❑ This will mean a radical life change for me, but I choose obedience over my own desires.

2. Trust God.

Think about it: You may be thinking, *Great, that means I have only three options for guys to date.* Although you may not know many Christian guys now, that doesn't mean that you will never meet any. God will bring the right person into your life when He is ready. Will you trust Him by walking according to His standards?

What does the Word say? Read Proverbs 3:5–6. Why do you think we are told to lean not on our own understanding? _____

_____

What's your experience? What practical steps can you take to acknowledge Him in all your ways when it applies to your dating life? _____

_____

_____

What do you think? According to this passage, what is the benefit of trusting and acknowledging God? _____

_____

_____

The more we trust in God's goodness, the easier it is to wait for His timing. Why do you think this is true? _____

_____

3. Avoid sexual immorality.

What does the Word say? Read 1 Thessalonians 4:3–5. If you are look-ing for God's will, He states it in this passage. What is His will for you? _____

_____

Think about it: In what ways could you avoid sexual immorality?_____

_____

_____

The Bible is clear that any sexual activity before marriage is sin. We are not to draw a line and see how close we can come to that line; instead, we must stay as far away from sinful behavior as possible. This means we should avoid all tempting situations.

Safety in Standards

What do you think? What are some boundaries you can set now that will help you avoid tempting situations later? _____

_____

_____

_____

✔ **Try This:** Take some time to think about the boundaries you will set for your dating life. Remember, good boundaries always line up with the Word of God. You may decide you won't be alone with a guy. If you don't have a "curfew," you might want to set one for yourself—and honor it. The more decisions you make to protect your purity, the easier it will be. On a date is not the time to determine your boundaries. They need to be decided long before your date picks you up. Boundaries may seem limiting now, but the rewards they bring are limitless.

Write your list of boundaries down and place them where you will see them often. Next, share them with a parent or trusted adult and ask that person to hold you accountable for living according to those standards.

✝ **Living the Word:** In order to stay pure, you must know how to battle temptation. Some think they can overcome it with sheer will power, while others say victory is impossible.

• Read 1 Corinthians 10:12–13 to see what God's Word says about temptation.

What warning is given in verse 12? _____

_____

_____

How can you apply this verse to your dating life? _____

_____

_____

_____

• We are all tempted at times, but the true test of someone who walks with God is how she responds to temptation. Verse 13 says that God provides a "way out" from temptation.

What do you think this phrase means? _____

_____

_____

_____

• Have you ever been in a tempting situation and taken the way out? If so, describe that experience. _____

_____

_____

_____

_____

Safety in Standards

If not, what will you do differently the next time? _____

_____

_____

_____

_____

_____

Dear Point Of Grace,

The other day somebody from school asked me if I was still a virgin in a way that made me feel bad for being one. My parents tell me all the time that waiting for marriage is what God wants me to do, but they aren't my age, and they have no clue what I have to go through each day. I have a boyfriend, and he and I have kissed, but that's all. There have been a few times when both of us wanted to do more than kiss, but I just didn't feel right about it, so we stopped.

But I'm so confused! Everything on TV seems to say that it's OK to have sex before marriage, and it's like people don't even think anything is wrong with sex before marriage. My body is telling me one thing, but my mind and my heart are trying to say something else. How can I have these feelings and still wait until I'm married?

Amy

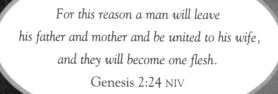

*For this reason a man will leave
his father and mother and be united to his wife,
and they will become one flesh.*
Genesis 2:24 NIV

Sex As God Designed It

Do you remember the first time you learned about sex? I imagine that many of you learned about it earlier than I did. I saw "those films" in the fifth grade that talked about sex and about the whole menstrual cycle. My mother also had "the talk" with me around that same time. It was fairly vague, and I remember thinking, *Ugh! I don't want to hear this from my mother!* It all seemed rather gross.

I also remember being at a conference for teens when I was thirteen. The speaker talked about French kissing and touching, and I leaned over and said to my best friend, "I will *never* do that!" However, as my hormone levels started to change, the other gender began to look rather interesting. Why? Because God created men and women to come together as husband and wife and to become one flesh.

The First Love Story. Genesis 2 records the account of the first man and woman ever in the world. It's really a beautiful story. Take a minute to read it. If you've read it before, try to read it fresh and imagine what it must have been like for them.

> The LORD God took the man and put him in the Garden of Eden to work it and take care of it....
>
> The LORD God said, "It is not good for the man to be alone. I will make a helper suitable for him."
>
> Now the LORD God had formed out of the ground all the beasts of the field and all the birds of the air. He brought them to the man to see what he would name them; and whatever the man called each living creature, that was its name. So the man gave names to all the livestock, the birds of the air and all the beasts of the field.
>
> But for Adam no suitable helper was found. So the LORD God caused the man to fall into a deep sleep; and while he was sleeping, he took one of the man's ribs and closed up the place with flesh. Then the LORD God made a woman from the rib he had taken out of the man, and he brought her to the man.
>
> The man said, "This is now bone of my bones and flesh of my flesh; she shall be called 'woman,' for she was taken out of man." For this reason a man will leave his father and mother and be united to his wife, and they will become one flesh.
>
> The man and his wife were both naked, and they felt no shame. (verses 15, 18–25 NIV)

Sex as God Designed It

Isn't that a beautiful love story? Can you imagine the wonder they felt as they first discovered each other? And notice that man was not complete until woman was created. Ah…we are special, indeed. The New American Standard Bible says in verse 22 that we were "fashioned" from Adam's rib. No wonder we like shopping so much; we were in "fashion" from the very beginning.

God made man from the dust of the ground, but He chose to make woman from the man's bone and flesh to symbolize that they were one flesh. The fact that we females were created from man does a lot to explain why we yearn to be in relationship with the opposite sex. Men and women are linked in a very special way. God said that men and women, when they are united together, actually become one flesh.

The Mystery of Married Love. So you see, sex was God's idea. God has given us a beautiful gift in sex, but He firmly restricts it to marriage. The Book of Ephesians gives us an amazing insight into marriage: It tells us that marriage symbolizes Christ's relationship with His church. Ephesians 5:31 quotes Genesis 2:24 ("For this reason a man will leave his father and mother and be united to his wife, and the two will become one flesh" NIV), then goes on to say, "This is a great mystery, but it is an illustration of the way Christ and the church are one" (verse 32 NLT).

God's plan is that sex in marriage show us a picture of what our relationship with Him can be—perfect oneness. He made man and woman a perfect fit so that when they come together there is nothing between them. God wants our relationship with Him to be like that.

In the book *Mystery of Marriage*, Mike Mason says, "For in touching a person of the opposite sex in the most secret place of his or her body, with one's own most private part, there is something that reaches beyond touch, that gets behind flesh itself to the place where it connects with spirit." So you see, physical intimacy is more than skin deep; it connects us on a spiritual level—a level that is reserved only for marriage.

Genesis 2:25 says that they were both naked and felt no shame. Oh my, did I say "naked"? Isn't that a bad thing? It wasn't supposed to be. Not in God's creation. You see, before man and woman sinned, everything was perfect. They weren't just physically naked, but their hearts and souls were also open to each other as well. Communication, openness, and honesty were not problems. God designed marriage to help fulfill our needs for intimacy and closeness.

Perfection Spoiled. But things didn't stay perfect for long. After Adam and Eve sinned, things began to change. They blamed each other. They hid from God because they were embarrassed of their nakedness.

And after that, things went from bad to worse. In the New Testament, the apostle Paul said, "They knew God, but they wouldn't worship Him as God or even give Him thanks. And they began to think up foolish ideas of what God was like. The result was that their minds became dark and confused. So God let them go ahead and do whatever shameful things their hearts desired. As a result, they did vile and degrading things with each other's bodies" (Romans 1:21, 24 NLT).

Sex as God Designed It

Sound familiar? Isn't that what much of America is doing? No wonder we get so confused about sex.

Confusing Messages about Sex. So, if sex is from God, why do we often think of it as dirty or nasty? Unfortunately, our world has taken one of the most beautiful parts of God's creation and misused it for selfish reasons. There are so many different views about sex that it can be rather confusing. Plus, many of the ideas are so conflicting that it really makes it hard to figure it all out. Here are some different views that I'm aware of. Do any seem familiar to you? "Everyone is doing it." "Only bad girls enjoy sex." "Honey, just wait till you've been married twenty years. It gets *old!*" "A truly 'sexy' girl will get turned on instantly." "Boys and girls are naturally perfect lovers. They know exactly what to do." "Kisses are always perfect and romantic."

Or, worse, you may hear *nothing at all*. It's no wonder we don't know what to think.

I am sorry that some adults downplay or talk bad about sex in their marriages, because it's awesome and should be enjoyed. Maybe one reason that sex outside of marriage seems so exciting is that the unmarried are the only ones talking about it. (I'm not saying that people should share their juicy details, but it would be nice to hear how much fun marriage is.)

"Fix your thoughts on what is true and honorable and right. Think about things that are pure and lovely and admirable. Think about things that are excellent and worthy of praise" (Philippians 4:8 NLT). Let's stop thinking about sex as something that is forbidden and naughty and start thinking about how awesome it will be someday when you've waited for a godly man and for your wedding night.

A Steamy Love Story. There is a book in the Bible that can compete with any romance novel you could ever read. However, you rarely hear sermons or talks about this book. I think it's because we are embarrassed to talk about the beauty of "sex" in church. Instead, we hear, "Don't do it. It's forbidden." I believe that God put this book in His Word for a purpose. The Song of Solomon is a descriptive story about the love between a man and a woman.

Solomon says to his future bride, "You are a garden locked up, my sister, my bride; you are a spring enclosed, a sealed fountain" (Song of Songs 4:12 NIV). He found her especially beautiful because no one else had trespassed in her garden. It had been saved for him to enjoy. He delighted in her love: "Your love is more delightful than wine" (1:2 NIV).

Love and sex are supposed to be delightful. God wants us to find that one person about whom we can say, "My lover is mine and I am his" (Song of Songs 2:16 NIV). And that person is to know you like no one else knows you. My precious husband, Stu, knows my deepest secrets. He not only knows what makes me laugh or cry, but he has seen and done things with me that no one else has. It's a bond that is right. Don't spoil the intimacy you are to have with your husband alone by sharing it with someone else.

We are also warned several times in Song of Solomon "not to awaken love until the time is right" (2:7; 3:5; 8:4 NLT). These verses remind us that in a time of weakness you can spoil the beautiful relationship God has prepared for you. You are so special and so unique. Don't give away and mess up what God created for you to enjoy.

True Love. What is true love anyway? First Corinthians 13:4–7 tells us exactly what love is like: "Love is patient and kind. Love is not jealous or boastful or proud or rude. Love does not demand its own way. Love is not irritable, and it keeps no record of when it has been wronged. It is never glad about injustice but rejoices whenever the truth wins out. Love never gives up, never loses faith, is always hopeful, and endures through every circumstance" (NLT).

Examine any relationship you now have or may have in the future in light of this definition of love. If you are truly in love, you will be "patient," as Scripture says, and wait for God and His timing. If your boyfriend loves you, he will not pressure you, and he will wait, too. If he pressures you and is not patient in his love for you, then maybe he is not the one for you.

Remember that "Love does not demand its own way." Isn't "making out" all about getting your or his own way? And true love "rejoices whenever truth wins out." The truth is that God loves you more than you can ever understand. He knows the very best for you.

Just the other day, as I told my son Price—for the fifty millionth time—to stop trying to climb into the fireplace, I thought, *Why do I continually tell him that?* It was an easy question to answer: Because I love him and know that he could get burned. Why do you think God continually warns us about sex outside of marriage? Because He knows how dangerous it is. Let's stop playing with fire. OK?

Worth the Wait. Your time will come if you will just hold out. I promise it will be worth the wait. All four of us waited until we were married to have sex. If we were able to wait, so can you! I honestly believe that one of the reasons so many marriages break up is that more and more couples have sex before they get married, and they later wonder whether they were ever truly in love or if their attraction was purely physical.

I'll never forget hearing Heather talk about her spiritual struggles before she met Brian. She was going through a difficult time of questioning. The three of us were happily married, and she didn't even have a prospect. One day, on her knees, crying out to the Lord, she finally came to the realization that God wanted some special time with just her. She made the choice to focus on and nurture her relationship with Him. And, of course, not too soon after that, Brian came into the picture.

I'm often amazed at how God works. Look back to Adam and Eve. "For Adam no suitable helper was found." But God had a plan all along. God put Adam into a deep sleep and gave him the perfect mate. I am just as guilty as you may be of trying to make things happen instead of trusting the Lord and waiting on Him. It's not always easy to wait—I know Heather would testify to that. But she would also testify that God was right in the end.

my heart is set on you

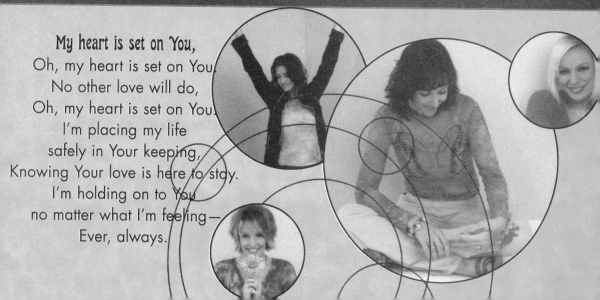

My heart is set on You,
Oh, my heart is set on You.
No other love will do,
Oh, my heart is set on You.
I'm placing my life
safely in Your keeping,
Knowing Your love is here to stay.
I'm holding on to You
no matter what I'm feeling—
Ever, always.

Your Wedding Night

📖 **Opening Scripture:** Please begin by reading James 1:17. Ask God to teach you from His Word today.

❁ **Sex—A Gift from God:** You have probably dreamed about your wedding day a thousand times. Most girls love to plan and envision what that day will be like. What kind of dress will you wear? What will your cake look like? How many bridesmaids will you have? If you are like most girls, you will change your mind a hundred times before that day arrives.

For all the dreaming about your wedding day, how often have you dreamed about your wedding night? Did you know that God designed that night to be like no other in your life? He planned for the wedding night between a man and woman to be like a gift they unwrap from one another. He planned for sex to be that gift.

Fill in the blanks: Fill in the missing words from James 1:17: "Every _____ and _____ gift is from above, coming down from the Father of heavenly lights, who does not change like shifting shadows."

What's your experience? Do you like gifts? If you're like most people, you love to receive gifts, both large and small. Who doesn't like to unwrap a pretty package to see what surprise is waiting for her?

Your Wedding Night

What is the best gift you ever received and why? _____

_____

_____

_____

_____

_____

Think about it: While earthly gifts are fun and brighten our days, they in no way compare to the kind of gifts God gives. His gifts surpass our wildest imaginations. They're what we would have asked for if we would have known what to ask for. He made us, so He knows the exact gift that will bring us the most joy.

Sex is a gift from God. He created it for a bride and groom to unwrap on their wedding night and not a day before.

Pray about it: Ask God to help you remember that His ways are always best and His gifts are perfect.

❧ Sex Outside of Marriage

Fill in the blanks: Read Hebrews 13:4 and fill in the missing words: "Marriage should be _____ by all, and the marriage_____ kept _____, for God will judge the adulterer and all the _____ immoral."

What do you think? According to this verse, how serious is the sin of sex before marriage?

❏ God really doesn't care as long as people love each other.

❏ God takes it very seriously and judges those who disobey Him.

❏ God understands that times have changed and allows people to make their own rules.

❏ God isn't concerned about this area of my life.

Think about it: This passage is one of many that deals with sexual immorality. The term "the marriage bed" refers to sexual activity. The Bible is explicitly clear about the matter. We are to wait until marriage before we have sex.

Abstinence until marriage is not a popular decision in our culture. The word *virgin* is laughed at on TV and in the movies. Those committed to purity are constantly pressured to change their decision.

What's your experience? Has there ever been a time when you were laughed at or pressured because of your commitment to stay sexually pure? If so, how did that experience make you feel? _____

_____

_____

_____

❧ Consequences of Sexual Sin

Fill in the blanks: Read Proverbs 6:32 and fill in the missing words: "But a man who commits adultery lacks_____; whoever does so _____ himself."

Your Wedding Night

What do you think? What are some ways that sexual sin can cause one to destroy herself? _____

_____

_____

Think about it: The consequences for sexual sin are devastating. You may know someone who has become pregnant or contracted a sexually transmitted disease. Often the most serious consequences are the unseen scars on the heart. This isn't to say God can't forgive someone; He will forgive her, but He doesn't remove the consequences of sin.

❧ Commit to Purity

Think about it: Will you commit to remaining sexually pure? If so, what are some practical steps you can take to make sure you wait? _____

_____

_____

It may not be the easiest decision you make, but it is well worth it. You may want to take offensive measures that will strengthen you to overcome temptation. The big decision to wait until marriage is reinforced by the many little decisions you make from day to day.

What do you think? List some benefits of sexual purity. _____

_____

_____

_____

_____

What's your experience? One important offensive step is to avoid tempting situations. If you do find yourself in a situation where you are being tempted, do you leave immediately? Why or why not? _____

_____

_____

_____

_____

_____

❧ Guard Your Heart

What does the Word say? Read Proverbs 4:23. What command does God give us in this passage? _____

_____

What do you think? What are some practical ways that you can do this?

- ❏ Wear a shield over my heart.
- ❏ Be careful about the things that I allow to influence me.
- ❏ Don't watch any TV at all.
- ❏ Bury all of my romantic feelings.

Think about it: Have you ever noticed how girls are careful in so many areas of life but absolutely careless when it comes to their hearts? God knows that our hearts are fragile, so He warns us to guard them.

Your Wedding Night

What's your experience? How seriously do you take the command to guard your heart?

- ❏ I have been careless in the past, but I am going to change after today.
- ❏ Because I have been hurt in the past, I now know that I must take it seriously.
- ❏ I have been cautious, knowing that my heart is fragile and easily broken.
- ❏ The more I grow in Christ, the more I am growing in this area.

Pray about it: Ask God to help you guard your heart as you wait for Him to bring your husband to you one day. How specifically will you ask Him to help you? _____

_____

_____

✔ **Try This:** Find the prettiest piece of paper you have. Now go to a place where you can be alone for a while. Write a letter to your future husband. You may want to tell him what you are feeling and thinking right now. Tell him that you are committed to staying sexually pure from this day on. Share with him your desire to give him the gift of your purity on your wedding night. After you finish the letter, date it and seal it in an envelope. Now put it in a safe place. Save that letter until your wedding night when you give it to your husband.

✝ Living the Word

• What if you have already participated in sexual activity? Are you exempt from God's blessings? Absolutely not. God offers His forgiveness to those who ask Him.

• Read I John 1:9. What promise does God give us if we confess our sins to Him? _____

_____

• This passage doesn't say that He might forgive us, but rather that He will. Will you claim this promise and choose to believe Him? If so, write a prayer thanking Him for His forgiveness. _____

_____

_____

_____

_____

• He promises to purify us from all unrighteousness. First John 1:9 doesn't say "some" unrighteousness, but "all." That means that when He forgives us, He forgives completely. We are made pure again.

• Will you ask Him to forgive you today? He longs to restore you and to strengthen you to walk in purity from this day forward.

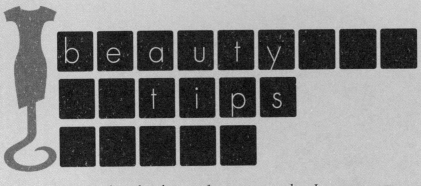

beauty tips

❀ Drink eight glasses of water every day. It helps your skin and keeps you healthy. Fill eight, eight-ounce (or four sixteen-ounce) bottles of water each day, and when you drink them all—you're done!

❀ Don't try to squeeze your body into clothes that are too small. Tight clothes only emphasize figure problems. Wear clothes that fit, and you'll be amazed by how great you can look.

❀ Makeup only looks as good as your skin underneath. Take good care of your skin.

❀ Sunscreen is a must—it is the best thing you can do to keep your skin beautiful year-round! Avoid tanning. Instead, choose a good sunless tanning lotion to get that sun-kissed look.

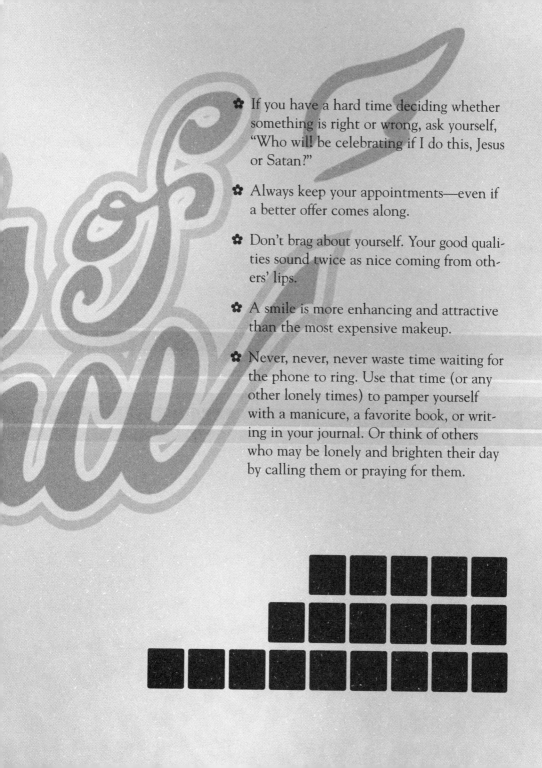

✿ If you have a hard time deciding whether something is right or wrong, ask yourself, "Who will be celebrating if I do this, Jesus or Satan?"

✿ Always keep your appointments—even if a better offer comes along.

✿ Don't brag about yourself. Your good qualities sound twice as nice coming from others' lips.

✿ A smile is more enhancing and attractive than the most expensive makeup.

✿ Never, never, never waste time waiting for the phone to ring. Use that time (or any other lonely times) to pamper yourself with a manicure, a favorite book, or writing in your journal. Or think of others who may be lonely and brighten their day by calling them or praying for them.

Girls Of Grace
the new worship album
from Point Of Grace,
featuring special guests
Jaci Velasquez, Jill Phillips,
Out of Eden, Joy Williams,
Rachael Lampa, Nichole Nordeman,
Jennifer Deibler of FFH,
Christy Nockels of Watermark

Girls Of Grace Journal
Spiral, ISBN 1-58229-269-8